Guide to
Naturopathy

D1328895

**GEDDES &
GROSSET**

Published by Geddes & Grosset, an imprint of
Children's Leisure Products Limited

© 1999 Children's Leisure Products Limited,
David Dale House, New Lanark ML11 9DJ, Scotland

First printed 1999
Reprinted 1999

Cover photograph by Spencer Jones, courtesy of
the Telegraph Colour Library

ISBN 1 85534 936 1

Printed and bound in the UK

Contents

Origins and Principles of Naturopathy

As the name suggests, naturopathy is very much connected with nature or things natural, and this is reflected in its previous name, nature cure. Indeed, remedies that anyone may practise as a matter of course, almost as instinct, can be called naturopathy. For example, fasting to relieve the symptoms of an upset stomach, bathing an aching joint or eating a sensible balanced diet to maintain good health are all examples of naturopathy. However, naturopathy is much more than this, as will become apparent.

The origins of the practice can be traced back well over two thousand years to the time of Hippocrates, the Greek physician. He became known as the 'father of medicine' and had as his basic premise the principle that no harm should be done, that is, any therapy administered should not create additional burdens for an already weakened or deficient body. Cures were therefore meant to work with the body and natural treatments were preferable. In addition, it was considered particularly important that a healthy diet and regular exercise be maintained. Hippocrates and his colleagues considered disease to be an effect of some imbalance and they sought a cause in the elements (air, water, etc) and other natural factors such as food. It is likely that this system of healing was practised by other cultures, including the Chinese, Indians and North American native peoples.

The basis of the modern practice can be traced back to the beginning of the 19th century and people such as Preissnitz, who used the beneficial effects of water as a therapy and thereby started what is now known as hydrotherapy, an important aspect of naturopathy. Preissnitz was a therapist in Germany, and towards the end of the 19th century in Bavaria, Father Kneipp, a monk, was obviously a naturopath in deed if not in name. He treated an American Benedictine by the name of Lust. Presumably as a result of his recovery, Lust stayed with Kneipp to study his particular methods of healing, and upon returning to the United States, he established his own form of natural medicine, which he called naturopathy. Thus, at the beginning of the 19th century, naturopathy began to be formally recognised. However, the term naturopathy was probably created by a Dr Scheel of New York City a few years earlier. The blend of therapies employed by Lust was varied and in the main holds good for the practice of naturopathy today. Included were nutrition and natural diet, homeopathy, herbal medicine, hydrotherapy, chiropractic (particularly involving the spine), and the management of stress.

Lust wrote numerous articles and books on the subject in

which he stressed the importance of the natural system for combating disease. In his programme of naturopathic cure, Lust advocated stopping all bad habits, among which he included overeating, the consumption of alcohol, meat, tea and coffee, and other similar excesses. Before considering a new lifestyle, corrective habits had to be introduced, such as exercising and breathing in the proper manner and, in general, a moderate approach taken to all things. The new lifestyle was then based upon certain principles which propagated and extended the corrective habits, namely good diet and fasting; osteopathy and chiropractic; steam, mud and 'light and air' baths; mineral salts, and much more. The fundamental healing force was considered to be nature itself, that is, the power of the individual to defeat disease. This is encapsulated in the phrase *vis medicatrix naturae*, the 'healing power of nature'.

In the early 1900s, naturopathy developed rapidly in the United States, but then from the mid-1930s the general picture of medicine changed appreciably. Technology developed on all fronts, and there were parallel advances in drugs and surgery and a jettisoning of antiquated practices such as mercury dosing. As a result, the type of medicine with which most of us are now familiar – allopathic medicine, treating by conventional means where drugs have the opposite effects to the symptoms manifested – became the dominant system of treatment.

Guide to Naturopathy

Naturopathic principles	Conventional approach	Comments
Treat the whole person – the holistic approach. A person is recognised as being a complex amalgamation of physical, mental, intellectual and emotional factors, all of which govern the state of health. Treatment must promote and work in harmony with all of these to bring about an improvement in health and wellbeing. No disease is completely out of reach.	Symptoms of the illness or condition, i.e. physical factors alone are the most important feature. In modern medical practice, the pace is frenetic and there is usually little time to consider anything other than the presenting symptoms.	While conventional medicine recognises the importance of mental, intellectual and emotional factors – having a positive attitude – in influencing recovery, it is usually considered less significant than the active treatment being given.
Any treatment given must *assist* the body's innate ability to restore good health, and aid inbuilt healing forces.	Drugs used may override the natural healing processes and dictate the route and rate of recovery.	Naturopathic remedies are gentle, non-irritant and nontoxic. Some conventional remedies are synthetic, highly potent substances which, while suppressing the original symptoms, may leave side effects in their wake.
The underlying root cause of a condition, of which symptoms are an expression, must be investigated and treated. There is no attempt to suppress symptoms which are regarded as part of the body's natural healing process and which may spring from mental and emotional factors as well as physical causes. Symptoms which would not be suppressed include minor fevers and headaches, slight digestive complaints and inflammation.	The underlying cause is sought but immediate treatment is often aimed at suppressing symptoms. If no physical cause is found, most patients, rightly or wrongly, end up feeling guilty if there is an emotional or mental cause for their symptoms. It is, of course, right that acute and painful symptoms should be relieved effectively and quickly.	The contrast is most apparent in the treatment of common minor ailments. There is a patient-led demand for instant relief from symptoms, engendered over the years by a widespread belief in the omnipotence of medicine and science. The medical profession acknowledge that this has led, firstly, to the wrongful over-prescription of drugs which has caused such problems as antibiotic resistance. Secondly, in many cases doctors are prepared to admit that their treatment has done little good in such minor cases, and that patients could have got better on their own!

Naturopathic principles	Conventional approach	Comments
Treatment must never cause harm or the appearance of side effects.	Side effects are a recognised feature of many conventional drug treatments, even if they are effective in relieving the symptoms of the complaint.	The use of naturopathic methods provides a successful treatment for many conditions without recourse to drugs which may in themselves cause harm.
Naturopathy is a system of promoting positive good health, brought about by such factors as changes in diet and lifestyle as well as in various treatment regimes. It is preventative medicine at its best.	Conventional medicine also seeks to promote good health but generally, only sees people once they have already become sick.	There is considerable common ground in the recognition of the main factors (diet, lifestyle, etc.) which promote good health. However, conventional medicine has been slow to recognise the value of some naturopathic methods, although this position is now changing.
Naturopaths are health specialists who are able to recommend treatment methods for specific complaints. Of equal importance, however, is their role in educating people in how to take charge of their own good health, instead of waiting until something goes wrong.	Most conventionally trained medical practitioners only have time to treat rather than to teach. Health education is, on the whole, the province of other specialists working alongside doctors.	Naturopaths would probably regard themselves as being in partnership with their patients with the aim of restoring and maintaining good health. The naturopath necessarily needs to know a great deal about all aspects of a patient's life. It is difficult for hard-pressed doctors to see the person behind the symptoms. Also, many feel uncomfortable with anything other than the 'doctor knows best' philosophy. It is for the doctor to dispense wisdom, medication and treatment and for the patient to follow this without question. People may feel inhibited about asking questions or raising concerns which seem to challenge medical advice. These attitudes are, however, changing.

The fundamentals of naturopathy

Naturopathy is thus a combination of different methods of natural healing but, more importantly, it is also a way of life. Also, of fundamental importance, is the fact that the naturopathic lifestyle should be viewed as a method of disease prevention. It is particularly important in helping to prevent the onset of many common conditions which most people are conditioned to accept as being inevitable. Examples include headaches, the common cold, essential hypertension (high blood pressure of unknown cause), peptic ulcers and many of the disorders associated with ageing, including maturity-onset diabetes and atherosclerosis. Many of these conditions are related to an unhealthy, Western lifestyle, particularly a diet high in fat, salt and refined carbohydrates, a sedentary existence lacking regular exercise, smoking, excess consumption of alcohol and high stress levels. It is encouraging to note that conventional medicine has, at long last, realised that it shares common ground with naturopathy in its recognition of such matters. Indeed, many medical practitioners now openly acknowledge that many of the factors which influence the maintenance of good, or the development of poor health are under individual control – a founding principle of naturopathy! Further, both conventional medicine and naturopathy share the aim of educating people about adopting the type of lifestyle which is conducive to good health. However, they continue to differ widely in their approach to the treatment of disorders and illnesses and in the underlying principles involved.

The principles of naturopathy are outlined below and compared and contrasted with those of conventional medicine, recognising common ground where this exists.

Therapeutic methods of naturopathy

The treatment methods of naturopathy are extremely wide-ranging, and a practitioner may become a specialist in one particular area. They are briefly outlined below and then the core elements are covered in more detail under their particular headings in the text.

(1) Nutrition and diet, including the use of vitamin and mineral supplements when necessary – in examining the cause of a disease or condition, a naturopath may well identify a particular mineral or other deficiency as a contributory factor. Hence in the naturopathic treatment of ailments, supplements are frequently recommended. A naturopathic diet for healthy people is based on wholefoods, i.e. those that are unrefined and as near to their natural state as possible. This type of diet is universally recommended by nutritionists for healthy eating in people who are well.

(2) Detoxification – the use of short periods of fasting or controlled diets and supplements to aid the natural processes by which the body rids itself of toxic substances.

(3) Methods to control and reduce stress – including recognising and eliminating the causes whenever possible, exercise, relaxation techniques, modification of diet and the use of supplements, particularly to support the adrenal gland.

(4) Hydrotherapy – the use of water to promote healing, possibly including colonic irrigation.

(5) Herbal medicine – the use of plants and their natural products to promote healing.

(6) Homeopathy – a method of healing using minute quantities of natural substances, based upon the principle that 'like cures like'.

(7) Physical therapies including massage, chiropractic, osteopathy and cranial osteopathy, therapeutic exercises and soft tissue manipulation such as rolfing –it may involve the use of various diagnostic and other equipment such as X-rays, ultrasound and diathermy. Iridology is frequently used as a diagnostic technique.

(8) Counselling and lifestyle alteration which may be of particular value in relieving psychological, behavioural and emotional problems, as well as physical ailments – treatment may include hypnotherapy, relaxation techniques and the use of imagery, with suggested adjustments in daily living. Other helpful measures may include colour, music and dance therapy.

(9) Acupuncture and oriental therapies – such as shiatsu, yoga and T'ai Chi Ch'uan.

(10) Exercise – the importance of exercise in the promotion of good health and in the treatment of ailments is recognised by naturopaths and forms a part of most programmes of therapy.

It is evident from the above that the full scope of naturopathy is extremely broad and one individual is unlikely to be an expert in all its disciplines. Also, the emphasis varies somewhat depending upon the country in which it is practised. The core elements, used by naturopaths everywhere, are diet, nutrition (including supplements and detoxification), stress management, herbal remedies, physical therapies, exercise, counselling and lifestyle modification and hydrotherapy. These are described below. In the UK, most naturopaths have completed a four year course at the British College of Naturopathy and Osteopathy which entitles them to use the initials MRN after their name. They have gained a diploma in naturopathy (ND) and may also hold one in osteopathy (DO). Physical therapies, along with diet, nutrition and lifestyle are important elements of the course. Some naturopaths may then seek further training, for example in more detailed aspects of herbal medicine.

Diet and Nutrition

In recent years there has been a great deal of confusion about what constitutes a healthy diet. However, it is now universally recognised that the type of Western diet eaten by many people in the UK, which is high in saturated animal fat, cholesterol, salt, sugar and refined carbohydrates but low in fibre, is bad for health and is implicated in the development of several serious medical conditions. This type of diet is largely based on an over-consumption of meat, dairy products and highly processed foods, with the ill effects being compounded by lack of exercise, smoking and excess drinking of alcohol. Health experts, nutritionists and alternative therapists, including naturopaths, recommend a wholefood diet based on foods eaten in as natural a state as possible. A naturopathic diet can be best examined in the context of the needs of the human body for the various nutritional elements contained in food.

The human body requires food to provide energy for all life processes and for growth, repair and maintenance of cells and tissues, including those of the immune system, vital for warding off disease. Individual needs vary according to age and activity levels but, in general, men require proportionately more food than women because of their larger body size. Young, active people require more food than those who are elderly and more sedentary. In addition, slight internal differences exist between individuals who may outwardly appear comparable.

There are three main groups of substances contained in food which are needed by the body in differing amounts; carbohydrates, proteins and fats. In addition, the body requires fibre (derived from plants) which is highly significant in promoting good health and in preventing a number of life-threatening diseases. Vitamins and minerals are needed on a daily basis in small amounts, and these are supplied by eating a variety of different foods. However, naturopaths may recommend the use of natural supplements in the treatment of various diseases and conditions.

Carbohydrates

Carbohydrates are organic compounds which may be simple or complex, and their role is to provide an easily utilised source of energy for the body (measured in calories). All carbohydrates are composed of carbon, hydrogen and oxygen and are manufactured by plants. The simple forms are sugars, of which the most basic is glucose. All carbohydrates are eventually broken down by digestive processes into glucose, which is absorbed and utilised by the body in various ways. With sugars, this process is rapid and the resulting glucose is soon absorbed into the bloodstream. It may be used immediately, particularly if energy demands are high, as during vigorous exercise, and athletes often take glucose for this purpose. Glucose is required by red blood cells and is the main source of energy for the brain. Starches are more complex (polysaccharide) carbohydrates built up of chains of glucose molecules. They take longer to be broken down by digestive enzymes than sugars and hence provide a slower, more gradual supply of glucose. The body fluids generally contain enough reserves of glucose to meet the energy requirements for one day's activity. In conditions in which there is a lack of available glucose, the body is able to manufacture it in the liver by a biochemical process called gluconeogenesis. Glycerol (from fats) and amino acids (from proteins) are used as raw materials in this process. Conversely, excess glucose is converted by the liver into the complex (polysaccharide) carbohydrate, glycogen, (animal starch). This is stored particularly in liver and muscle cells and is used first when there is a lack of glucose in the blood.

In general, simple sugars, especially the refined type found in processed foodstuffs, e.g. sweets, biscuits, cakes, chocolates, sauces etc, merely provide the body with calories and are a significant cause of tooth decay. Starches, which are found in a wide range of foods, including cereals, grains, bread, pasta, potatoes, vegetables and fruits, are far more useful, often having accompanying fibre, vitamins and minerals. However, the levels of these are reduced in starchy foods that are refined and processed, e.g. white varieties of bread, flour, rice and pasta. Many people in the Western world consume only the unhelpful forms of refined sugars and carbohydrates which are easily eaten in excess and contribute towards the problems of tooth decay, weight gain and obesity. High sugar consumption also promotes the conditions leading to the development of atherosclerosis.

Naturopaths, in common with other nutritional experts, recommend that complex carbohydrates in the form of starchy foods should constitute 60–70 per cent of the overall daily intake of calories. These should be in the form of wholemeal bread, cereals, whole grains, brown rice and pasta and potatoes (especially with their skins), which have a high content of fibre as well as starch. They are more satisfying and filling than white varieties of the same foods and hence reduce the tendency to overeat. This aids both weight loss in obesity and maintenance of a correct body weight. Naturopaths may recommend a gradual changeover to these types of starchy foods as part of a programme of diet modification, so that white varieties are eventually replaced altogether.

Proteins

Proteins are the structural components of the body forming the basis of cells, tissues and organs. They are a large group of organic compounds consisting of carbon, hydrogen, nitrogen and oxygen atoms. These are arranged in various ways to form units called amino acids, which, when joined together in long chains, make up the structure of the protein. There are 20 basic amino acids, which are usually arranged in linear molecules known as polypeptides. Although there are only 20 different kinds, there are a huge number of possible arrangements in a polypeptide or protein, as the amino acids can be in any order. Most proteins consist of more than one polypeptide chain and there are many thousands in the human body, each with a unique structure but all made from the 'pool' of 20 amino acids. In addition to being structural molecules, proteins are used in the body for storage, as messengers (e.g. hormones), as carriers (e.g. the 'globin' in the haemoglobin of the blood which transports oxygen) and as catalysts of biochemical reactions (e.g. enzymes).

The body is capable of manufacturing 12 of the 20 amino acids. However, the remainder, called the 'essential amino acids', must be obtained from the diet. Proteins are widely found in foods derived both from plant and animal sources. Plant sources include beans, peas, pulses, whole grains, nuts and seeds, while red meat, poultry, fish, milk, cheese, yoghurt and eggs constitute the animal sources. Red meat is a good source of essential amino acids and iron, and is traditionally regarded as 'first class' protein. However, vegetarians can obtain plenty of both from plant sources and from dairy products. In fact, it is generally recommended that the consumption of red meat should be limited to once, or perhaps twice, a week, with chicken, fish, pulses, beans, etc, which are high in protein but low in saturated fat, chosen as alternatives. Proteins should only make up 10 to 15 per cent of the total calories in the daily intake of food. Naturopaths may recommend an increased consumption of plant-based protein and a reduced reliance on meat and dairy products. Oily fish (e.g. mackerel, herring, sardines, salmon, trout) are good sources both of protein and essential unsaturated oils. These are extremely important in the maintenance of good health and in the prevention of the development of heart disease. It is generally recommended by naturopaths and other nutritional experts that oily fish should be eaten two or three times each week. (*See also* Fats). Peas and beans, which are good sources of vegetable protein, should be included in the diet since it has been demonstrated that these can also act to reduce levels of blood cholesterol.

Fats

Fats are a group of organic compounds that occur naturally in plant and animal cells in the form of lipids, consisting of carbon, hydrogen and oxygen atoms. Lipids include oils, fats, waxes and related substances, known as 'derived lipids'. A fat consists of one glycerol and three fatty acid molecules, collectively known as a triglyceride, and, during digestion, is broken down into its constituent parts by enzymes called lipases. Fats play a vital role in the human body and perform many functions. They are an important energy store, having twice the calorific value (38 calories per gram) than carbohydrates. In human beings, fat is deposited in a layer beneath the skin (subcutaneous fat) where it provides insulation and cushioning. It is also laid down in deeper regions of the body (adipose tissue) around organs and within cells. Animal fat, including that of human beings, is solid at room temperature and is of the type known as saturated (*see* below).

Each fatty acid contains a long hydrophobic hydrocarbon chain (i.e. one that is not soluble in water) and a terminal carboxylic acid group (COOH) that is extremely hydrophilic (i.e. water-soluble). The chain lengths vary from 1 to nearly 30 carbon atoms and may be saturated or unsaturated. Saturated fats have all their available chemical bonds filled with hydrogen atoms and cannot join with other compounds. Unsaturated fats do not have the full complement of hydrogen atoms in their structure and have a softer or more liquid consistency.

Fatty acids have three major functions in the human body:

(1) They are the building blocks of phospholipids (lipids containing phosphate) and glycolipids (lipids containing carbohydrate). These molecules are vital components of the outer, surrounding membranes of all cells, controlling the passage of substances both inwards and outwards.

(2) Fatty acid derivatives, i.e. compounds that are made from them, serve as hormones and chemical messengers within and between cells.

(3) Fatty acids are stored within cells as triglycerides (i.e. joined to a glycerol molecule) as fuel reserves. They are

broken down when required to release large quantities of energy.

Saturated fats such as cholesterol are found in meat and dairy products, i.e. whole milk, cheese, butter and eggs. Many processed foods have saturated fats added to them and they are widely used in manufacturing. Saturated fatty acids are converted by liver cells into cholesterol, which is an important substance in the body, being a component of cell membranes and a precursor in the production of steroid (sex) hormones and bile salts. However, an excess level in the blood causes atheroma, or furring of the arteries, which is a causal factor in angina, strokes and various forms of heart disease and is a feature of diabetes mellitus. Men and postmenopausal women in Western countries are at particular risk of premature death from strokes and heart disease. It has been proved that the diet in these countries, which is rich in saturated fat and hence cholesterol but low in protective substances (oily fish, vegetable oils containing linoleic and linolenic acid), is a major factor in this high level of mortality.

Unsaturated fats or oils are of two types: polyunsaturated and monounsaturated. Monounsaturated fats have one available site in the molecule to bond to a hydrogen atom. Sources include olive oil, rapeseed oil, groundnut oil and some fish oils. Polyunsaturated fats have several available sites for binding to hydrogen atoms in their molecular structure.

Sources include oily fish (mackerel, salmon, herring, trout), vegetable oils (corn, sunflower, safflower, grapeseed) and nuts and seeds such as walnuts and sesame seeds. Among the polyunsaturated group are those called the 'essential fatty acids', which human beings can obtain only from food. Important ones are linoleic and linolenic acid, which have been shown to lower the levels of triglycerides and cholesterol in the blood and decrease the tendency for clotting factors called platelets to clump together. High blood cholesterol and triglyceride levels and aggregation of platelets are all involved in the development of furring or blocking of the arteries (atheroma and atherosclerosis). Good sources of linoleic acids are soya bean, safflower, sunflower, corn and walnut oil. Good sources of linolenic acid are linseed, flaxseed, walnut and soya bean oil. The essential fatty acid contained in the fish oils mentioned above is called eicosapentaenoic acid or EPA.

Human blood contains substances called lipoproteins, which are molecules of proteins that carry fat. These are of two types: low density lipoproteins (LDL) and high-density lipoproteins (HDL). The relative ratio of LDL to HDL is crucial in the prevention or development of arterial disease. This is because HDL carries cholesterol to the liver where it is broken down and eventually eliminated. LDL, however, deposits cholesterol. In the presence of saturated fats and cholesterol, platelets are encouraged to aggregate, which leads to narrowing of the arterial lumen (internal space), facilitating the trapping and furring of the arteries by fat deposits. Linoleic and linolenic acid and EPA inhibit the clumping together of platelets. Studies have shown that people who naturally eat a diet rich in fish oils, such as the Japanese and Inuit (Eskimos), have very little heart disease. It is only if they change to the Western type of diet, rich in saturated animal fat and cholesterol, that their incidence of heart disease increases.

Hence, for those who are not vegetarians, a naturopath may recommend eating oily fish two or three times a week, particularly as a substitute for red meat. It is the overall ratio of HDL to LDL that is important, with the aim of keeping blood cholesterol at a low level. Other recommendations might therefore include using skimmed or semi-skimmed milk, eating low fat dairy products (cottage cheese, natural yoghourt, fat-reduced cheese), choosing chicken or white fish, and grilling or steaming rather than frying food. It may be advised to eat red meat very sparingly, if at all, and to reduce the consumption of eggs to no more than two each week. In addition, the healthy vegetable oils mentioned above should be used as much as possible but they must always be fresh and never rancid. The human body has the capacity to convert linolenic acid into EPA and so vegetarians can choose alternatives to fish oil. The richest source of linolenic acid is flaxseed oil, which also contains useful amounts of linoleic acid. EPA from fish oils and linolenic acid from flaxseed or linseed oil have the additional advantage of having anti-allergic and anti-inflammatory properties. Eczema, psoriasis, rheumatoid arthritis and menstrual symptoms are all conditions that have shown improvement in some people when intake of these oils has been increased.

The overall intake of fat in a healthy diet should not exceed 30 per cent of the total calories consumed, and this should largely be in the form of beneficial polyunsaturated types. Monounsaturated fats do not raise blood cholesterol levels and are also not thought to reduce them. It must also be remembered that diet alone cannot protect a particular person against heart disease. As is well known, lifestyle factors, particularly lack of exercise and smoking, are the other significant parts of the risk equation. It is also likely that genetic predisposition is important in some individuals.

Fibre

Fibre is derived from the cell walls of plants. In recent years, the presence or absence of sufficient quantities of dietary fibre has been recognised as one of the most significant causes of ill health, particularly in Western countries. Some of the diseases linked to a lack of dietary fibre are extremely serious or are a cause of severe discomfort and pain. Also, while some are directly linked to the digestive tract, others affect other body systems and organs so that a lack of dietary fibre can have far-reaching consequences. Diseases include:

(1) Digestive – bowel cancer (cancer of the large intestine –

colon or rectum), irritable bowel syndrome, constipation, diverticulosis.

(2) Heart and circulation (linked with high consumption of animal fats) – atherosclerosis, atheroma, varicose veins.

(3) Others – obesity, kidney stones (some cases), gallstones, diabetes mellitus (all linked with other dietary factors).

Once again, studies have shown that these conditions are rare in people eating a largely plant-based, wholefood diet. However, if these same people change to a Western diet that is low in dietary fibre, such diseases begin to appear.

Dietary fibre, also known as *roughage*, has various components, the most significant of which is cellulose, which forms the main part of plant cell walls. The most readily available sources are foods containing wholewheat bran, such as wholemeal flour and bread, brown pasta, rice and spaghetti. *Cellulose* cannot be digested directly by the human gut, although a certain amount of degradation is brought about by the natural population of bacteria in the colon. Cellulose is insoluble fibre, i.e. it does not break down in water. It is able to bind to water and this increases the weight and bulk of faeces and promotes a quicker passage through the large intestine. The other components of fibre are termed non-cellulose complex polysaccharides, i.e. they are carbohydrates.

Pectins are found in many fruits and peel, especially citrus rind, and in vegetables and their skins. The have gel-producing effects and are able to bind to cholesterol and bile salts in the intestine so that these substances are eliminated rather than absorbed. They are water-soluble and promote a slower release of food from the stomach and a longer time for nutrients to be absorbed. This has the effect of helping to prevent a sudden after-meal elevation in blood sugar, which is particularly important for people with diabetes. *Hemicelluloses* are found in oat bran, seeds, peas and beans, grains, vegetables and fruit. They are an important source of helpful short-chain fatty acids, which provide energy for the cells in the lining of the colon and are believed to have anti-cancer activity. Hemicellulose is soluble fibre that binds cholesterol and bile salts. (Eating oats, for example as porridge, has been shown to lower blood cholesterol levels and hence reduce the risk of atherosclerosis and heart disease. *See* Fats.)

Mucilages are found in seeds and beans, and one type, guar gum, obtained from an Indian crop plant, is widely used commercially in many food and non-food products. Mucilages remove cholesterol, delay the emptying of the stomach, and reduce after-meal peaks of glucose and insulin, which is particularly important in diabetes. They also act as natural laxatives. *Gums*, like pectins, are gel-forming substances and are soluble in water. One form, gum arabic, is widely used by the food industry and also acts as a natural laxative.

Lignin is a complex polymer that is found especially in the woody parts of plants but also in vegetables, fruit and grains. It possesses anti-microbial and anti-cancer properties. *Algal fibre* is primarily obtained from seaweeds and two well-known examples, agar and carrageenan, are widely used in food manufacturing. They are gelling agents that are water-soluble. Agar and alginate have the ability to reduce the absorption of heavy metal contaminants (which may be present in food) into the body. Carrageenan, however, has been shown to produce a number of deleterious effects in experiments with rats and is regarded with suspicion by naturopaths.

The health-promoting effects of eating a range of dietary fibre can be summarised as follows:

(1) The presence of fibre necessitates more thorough chewing of food and hence slows down eating. It produces a feeling of fullness more rapidly, and there is therefore less likelihood of overeating and weight gain.

(2) A high proportion of fibre delays the passage of food from the stomach into the intestine so that this becomes a gradual process. This reduces the 'peaking' of blood sugar levels that tends to occur after meals, resulting in a slower rise and provision of energy. This is very important in both the prevention and treatment of diabetes mellitus because of the effect on blood glucose and hence on the release of insulin.

(3) Fibre in the diet promotes a greater release of enzymes, hormones and secretions from the pancreas, which are vital in digestion and other metabolic processes.

(4) A high intake of soluble fibre removes cholesterol and triglycerides from the blood and promotes their excretion in the faeces. This is enormously beneficial in preventing arterial and heart disease.

(5) A high fibre diet speeds up the passage of food through the intestine and increases the bulk and weight of faeces as a result of absorption of water. The faster transit time means that there is a reduced exposure to harmful toxic or carcinogenic substances, which may be present in food or produced by gut bacteria. A larger bulk of faeces containing water passes more easily through the colon and reduces the likelihood of the formation of diverticulae (small sac-like pouches that can become inflamed – diverticulitis). Also, the stool is passed without straining at the anus, reducing the likelihood of the development of haemorrhoids.

(6) A high proportion of dietary fibre favours the growth of helpful, acid-loving bacteria in the colon at the expense of harmful species that produce endotoxins. These acid-loving bacteria are able to ferment the digested food partially, providing the body with helpful short-chain fatty acids, utilised by the liver, and energy which is made available to cells lining the colon. The short-chain fatty

acids, particularly butyrate, have been shown to possess anti-carcinogenic properties.

(7) As a result of a more effective passage and elimination of food waste, a high fibre diet helps to prevent the development of constipation and is an effective, safe and gentle form of treatment for this condition. In irritable bowel syndrome (IBS), there is an abnormally rapid passage of food through the digestive system, often producing alternating bouts of constipation and diarrhoea. In this case, the addition of suitable fibre of the water-soluble variety (vegetables and fruit, peas and beans) helps to stabilise the condition of the colon and restore a more normal rate of passage. (Wheat bran is considered by naturopaths to be unhelpful in the treatment of IBS, since it often plays a significant part in food intolerance and allergy, which may in itself be a cause of the condition.)

(8) Pectins, mucilages and algal polysaccharides help to remove harmful heavy metal contaminants from food by inhibiting their absorption into the body. Lignins are altered by beneficial, acid-loving bacteria in the colon to produce substances that have anti-carcinogenic and antioxidant properties.

Although the beneficial effects of eating a wide variety of plant fibres in the diet are well documented, some caution must be exercised. For example, except in the treatment of certain medical conditions, naturopaths would probably not recommend supplementing the diet with one particular form of dietary fibre. Also, eating supplementary wheat bran in this form alone is not generally recommended as this interferes with the absorption of minerals by the body and can result in deficiencies. The same may apply to whole, raw cereal grains, which, again, should be eaten in moderation as part of a high fibre diet. Grains that have been cooked, as in the manufacture of bread, do not have this effect. In general, an adult should try to eat about 30 g (or 10 oz) of fibre each day. This is easily achieved by eating cereals, wholemeal bread, brown rice and pasta, fruits, vegetables and salads (at least five portions daily), and pulses (lentils, beans, peas, etc). Many commercially produced snack foods, such as savoury biscuits, are high in fibre. However, these frequently contain significant quantities of fat and salt, and so are best eaten sparingly and not as a substitute for natural high fibre foods.

Vitamins

Vitamins are a group of organic substances that are required in minute quantities in the diet to maintain good health. They are involved in a large number of cellular processes, including growth and repair of tissues and organs, metabolism of food, and functioning of the immune, nervous, circulatory and hormonal systems.

There are two groups of vitamins: those that are fat-soluble, including A, D, E and K, and those that are water-soluble – C (ascorbic acid) and the B group. A lack of a particular vitamin may result in a deficiency disease. Water-soluble vitamins dissolve in water and cannot be stored in the body but must be obtained from the diet on a daily basis. Any excess is simply excreted. Fat-soluble vitamins (with the partial exception of D and K) are also obtained from food but any excess can be stored by the liver. Hence they are needed on a regular basis in order to maintain the body's reserves. However, excessive doses, particularly of A and D (usually arising as a result of taking too many supplements), can have toxic effects because of a buildup in the liver.

Vitamin A

Vitamin A, or *retinol*, is a fat-soluble vitamin that must be obtained from the diet. It has a vital role in maintaining the epithelial layers of the skin and mucous membranes so that these function effectively and produce their secretions. It is also needed for the manufacture of rhodopsin, a light-sensitive pigment, alternatively called visual purple, that is essential for vision in dim light. Good sources of vitamin A are orange and yellow vegetables and fruits, particularly carrots, peaches and apricots, and also green vegetables, eggs, dairy products (full fat), liver and fish oils. Vegetables, especially carrots, contain plant substances called carotenes or carotenoids, some of which are precursors of vitamin A, i.e. they can be converted into the vitamin. Carotenes such as beta-carotene have vital antioxidant properties, as does vitamin A itself. Because of its role in maintaining the health of the body's epithelial surfaces, vitamin A has also been shown to enhance the immune response by boosting the cells that fight infections and tumours. Deficiency of vitamin A causes night blindness and a deterioration in the health of mucous membranes and skin. This can cause increased respiratory and ear infections, and dry skin, with more susceptibility to skin conditions and dull, lifeless hair. A sustained lack of vitamin A contributes to the failure of a child to grow and thrive, and weight loss and general debility in people of any age. The RDA (recommended daily amount) is 0.75 mg but excessive doses should be avoided as these can cause toxic effects.

Vitamin B₁

Vitamin B₁ (*thiamine* or *aneurin*) is involved in carbohydrate metabolism and the vital provision of energy for all body processes. It is essential for the healthy functioning of the nervous system and muscles and is a water-soluble vitamin. It plays a part in the mechanisms that combat pain, and it may have a role in intellectual functions of the brain. Good sources of vitamin B₁ are whole grains, potatoes, brown rice, yeast, pulses, green vegetables, eggs, dairy products, liver, kidney, meat, chicken and fish. A slight deficiency causes digestive upset, sickness, constipation, tiredness, irritability and forgetfulness. Prolonged lack of thiamine causes the development of the deficiency disease beriberi, which occurs mainly in countries in which the staple diet is polished rice. This causes inflammation of nerves and results in fever, breathing difficulties, palpitations and possible heart failure and death. The recommended daily allowance (RDA) is 1–1.3 mg.

Vitamin B2

Vitamin B2 (*riboflavin*) is involved in carbohydrate metabolism in the enzyme reactions in cells and in the provision of energy. It also helps to maintain the health of the mucous membranes and skin. It is a water-soluble vitamin that must be obtained from food, and its sources are similar to those for thiamine. A deficiency may cause a sore, irritated tongue and lips, dry skin and scalp and possibly, nervousness, trembling, sleeplessness and giddiness. The RDA is 1.3–1.6 mg.

Vitamin B3

Vitamin B3 (*niacin, nicotinic acid*) is involved in the maintenance of healthy blood and circulation, the nervous system and functioning of the adrenal glands. It is a water-soluble vitamin and good sources include some cereals (excluding maize), peanuts, nuts, yeast, eggs, dairy products, peas, beans, dried fruits, globe artichokes, meat, kidney, liver and chicken. A deficiency causes sickness and diarrhoea, appetite loss, peptic ulcers, dermatitis, irritability, depression, sleeplessness, headaches and tiredness. In more severe cases, the deficiency disease pellagra arises, producing the symptoms listed above but with accompanying dementia. Pellagra usually arises in people eating a diet based on maize with an associated lack of animal protein and dairy products. Although maize contains nicotinic acid, it is in an unusable form and does not contain the essential amino acid tryptophan, which the body needs to utilise the acid. The RDA is 1.8 mg.

Vitamin B₅

Vitamin B₅ (*pantothenic acid*) is involved in the metabolism of carbohydrates and fats and in the maintenance of the nervous and immune systems and the function of the adrenal glands. It is widely found in all types of food and is also produced within the gut. Deficiency is not common, but low levels may be associated with the development of osteoarthritis and symptoms associated with poor adrenal gland function (headaches, tiredness, sleeplessness, sickness and abdominal pains), particularly at times of stress. The RDA is 4–7 mg.

Vitamin B₆

Vitamin B₆ (*pyroxidine*) is involved in the metabolism of certain amino acids and in the functioning of the immune system by the production of antibodies to combat infection. It is involved in the manufacture of red blood cells and in the metabolism of carbohydrates and fats. It is a water-soluble vitamin that is widely found in many foods. A deficiency may play a role in the development of atherosclerosis and depression of the immune system. The RDA is 1.5–2 mg.

Vitamin B$_9$

Folic acid, vitamin B$_9$, is necessary for the correct functioning of vitamin B$_{12}$ in the production of red blood cells and in the metabolism of carbohydrates, fats and proteins. It is a water-soluble vitamin, and good sources include liver, kidney, green vegetables, yeast, fruits, dried beans and pulses, whole grains and wheatgerm. A deficiency in folic acid is quite common and produces anaemia, tiredness, sleeplessness, forgetfulness and irritability. A good intake of folic acid is important for women trying to conceive and in maintaining a healthy pregnancy. A deficiency in folic acid is a common finding in women with cervical dysplasia (abnormality in cells of the cervix, which can be a precancerous condition) and in those taking oral contraceptives. In addition, it is commonly deficient in people suffering from some forms of mental illness, depression, Crohn's disease and ulcerative colitis. Elderly people are quite frequently found to have low levels of folic acid. The RDA is 0.3 mg.

Vitamin B$_{12}$

Vitamin B$_{12}$ (cyanocobalamin) is necessary for the correct functioning of folic acid and is important in the production of nucleic acids (genetic material), in the maintenance of the myelin (fatty) sheath surrounding nerve fibres and in the production of red blood cells. It is involved in the metabolism of proteins, carbohydrates and fats, and in the maintenance of healthy cells. It is a water-soluble vitamin that is found in dairy products, egg yolks, meat, liver, kidney and fish. Blood levels of vitamin B_{12} are often low in people suffering from Alzheimer's disease, as is also the case in some psychiatric illnesses. B_{12} deficiency results in anaemia, but often this is the result of faulty absorption of the vitamin rather than dietary lack. In order for the vitamin to be absorbed, a substance known as intrinsic factor must be produced, along with hydrochloric acid, by secretory cells in the stomach. When this mechanism is defective, the condition known as pernicious anaemia may arise. Prolonged B_{12} deficiency also causes severe degeneration of the nervous system, producing symptoms of tingling and numbness in the limbs, loss of certain reflexes and sensations, lack of coordination, speech difficulties, confusion, irritability and depression. In addition, there is pallor, tiredness, breathlessness and irregular heartbeat caused by the development of anaemia. The RDA is 2 micrograms.

Biotin

Biotin (*vitamin B complex*) is a water-soluble vitamin involved in the metabolism of fats, including the production of glucose in conditions in which there is a lack of available carbohydrates. It works in conjunction, although independently, with insulin and can be important in the treatment of diabetes. Good sources of biotin include egg yolk, liver, kidney, wheat and oats, yeast and nuts, and it is also synthesised by gut bacteria. Deficiency is very uncommon in adults but in young infants a lack of biotin may be a cause of seborrhoeic dermatitis (cradle cap). The RDA is 0.1–0.2 mg.

Vitamin C

Vitamin C (ascorbic acid), an important substance, is vital in the maintenance of cell walls and connective tissue and is essential for the health of blood vessels, cartilage, gums, skin, tendons and ligaments. It facilitates the uptake and absorption of iron, is involved in the immune system in fighting off infections and has antiviral properties. It also promotes the repair of wounds and has vital antioxidant activity. It is important in the correct functioning of the adrenal glands, especially at times of stress. Blood levels of vitamin C are often low in people suffering from asthma. Since it is involved in the control of cholesterol and the metabolism of fats, a dietary lack of vitamin C is significant in the development of atherosclerosis. The levels of vitamin C in the fluid (aqueous humour) and lens of the human eye are normally high but are low in people with cataracts. Levels are also low in women with cervical dysplasia (abnormal cells in the cervix, or neck of the womb) and people suffering from Crohn's disease or fistula (an abnormal opening between two hollow organs or between such an organ or gland and the exterior).

A study of men with hypertension (high blood pressure) revealed that they also had low blood levels of vitamin C. Because of its effects on cartilage and connective tissue, a lack of the vitamin is thought to be a contributory factor in the development and progression of osteoarthritis. Likewise, vitamin C is vital in preventing gum disease and in the repair of tendons, ligaments and connective tissues. Vitamin C is water-soluble and is found in fresh fruits (especially citrus and red and black berries) and vegetables. Levels decline when these foods are kept for any length of time or are subjected to heat, light and cooking, and so they are best eaten in a fresh, raw state whenever possible. A deficiency of vitamin C causes the development of scurvy, the symptoms of which include swollen, bleeding gums and loose teeth, subcutaneous bleeding (i.e. beneath the skin), numerous infections, tiredness, loss of muscle mass and strength, bleeding into joints, ulcers, anaemia, fainting and diarrhoea. Eventually the major organs are affected, and scurvy is eventually fatal if not treated. It is now uncommon and is easily prevented by adequate intake of vitamin C. Some of the symptoms may arise if dietary levels are low, however, as was reported quite recently in a teenage girl who was living on a diet of junk food and fizzy drinks. The RDA is 30 mg.

Vitamin D

Vitamin D occurs as two steroid derivatives: D_2, or *calciferol*, in yeast and D_3, or *cholecalciferol*, which is produced by the action of sunlight on the skin. Vitamin D is vital in the control of blood calcium levels, prompting an increased absorption of the mineral from the intestine so that there is a good supply for the production and repair of bones and teeth. In addition, vitamin D promotes the uptake of phosphorus. Good dietary sources of fat-soluble vitamin D are oily fish, such as mackerel, sardines, salmon and tuna and kippers, liver, egg yolk, fortified margarine and dairy produce. In addition, it is produced in the skin by the action of sunlight on a form of cholesterol (7–dehydrocholesterol). Vitamin D is converted by the liver and then the kidneys into a much stronger form called 1_125–dihydroxycholecalciferol. Hence some liver and kidney diseases can reduce the effective potency of vitamin D even when dietary levels are adequate.

It appears that in osteoporosis the conversion process by the kidneys is impaired in some cases, although the reasons for this are not totally clear. Deficiency in vitamin D is also quite common in people suffering from Crohn's disease and ulcerative colitis. A slight deficiency in vitamin D causes tooth decay, softening of the bones with consequent risk of injury, muscular cramps and weakness. More severe deficiency causes rickets in children and osteomalacia in adults. These conditions are characterised by soft bones that bend out of shape, causing deformity. The condition is particularly severe in children and may result in poor, stunted growth, but it is uncommon in Western countries since many foods are fortified with the vitamin. The RDA is 10 micrograms (0.1 mg) but excessive doses should be avoided as these can have toxic effects.

Vitamin E

Vitamin E comprises a group of fat-soluble compounds, called *tocopherols*, which are widely found in many foods. These are involved in sustaining the health of cell membranes and preventing damage and may be important in the process of ageing. Vitamin E helps to maintain the blood and skin and aids resistance to infection. Deficiency is rare in human beings, but may cause unhealthy skin and hair and be a factor in miscarriage and in prostate gland enlargement in men. The RDA is 10 mg.

Vitamin K

Vitamin K (*menadione*) is fat-soluble and is essential for the clotting of blood, being involved in the formation of prothrombin which, with calcium, is changed into thrombin during the coagulation process. The vitamin is manufactured by bacteria in the large intestine but is also found in liver, kidney, green vegetables, eggs, wholewheat and seaweed. Deficiency is rare in healthy persons but has been reported in those suffering from ulcerative colitis and

Crohn's disease. It may rarely occur if antibiotics have to be taken for a prolonged period, and symptoms include nosebleeds and subcutaneous bleeding. Vitamins K and C, given together, were reported in one study to relieve morning sickness in pregnant women. The RDA of vitamin K is 70–140 mg.

Minerals and trace elements

Minerals are chemical substances that are generally associated with non-living materials such as rocks and metals. However, forms of them are also found in all living things and they play a vital part in many metabolic processes. Some minerals, notably calcium and phosphorus, are present in significant amounts in the human body, mainly in bones and teeth. Others, for example iron, iodine and sodium, occur in extremely small quantities but are, nonetheless, very important substances within the body.

Minerals that are needed only in minute amounts are called *trace elements*. As with vitamins, a lack of a particular mineral can lead to a deficiency disease with the appearance of a set of symptoms that may develop over a long period of time. The effects of deficiency may be quite complex in some cases and, as with vitamins, the condition may arise either as a direct result of dietary insufficiency or be because of some malabsorption or other dysfunction within the body. Naturopaths are very concerned with the role played by minerals in the course of disease and may recommend supplements for the treatment of particular conditions (*see* examples later in text).

Some of the more important minerals are described below:

Sodium

Sodium is essential in minute quantities to ensure the correct functioning of nerves and as a vital constituent of cellular and tissue fluids. However, the quantities needed are, in normal circumstances, readily obtained from eating a balanced and varied diet. Most foods contain traces of sodium, usually in the form of sodium chloride or common salt. The problem for people, particularly those eating a Western diet, is an excessive intake of salt which can contribute towards a number of serious health problems.

These include high blood pressure, or hypertension, heart and circulatory disorders and strain on the kidneys, which can lead to the development of disease in these organs. In order to avoid this, no salt should be added to food either during cooking or at the table. It should also be remembered that almost all manufactured and processed foods have a high salt content. When such foods are used, the labels should be checked for salt content. Whenever possible, when these must be used, low-salt varieties should be chosen. Many people (and also animals) enjoy the taste of salt, which can enhance the flavour of food and also acts as a preservative. However, this is an acquired habit that can be broken, and it may be helpful to use herbs and spices as a substitute for salt in cooking. Salt substitutes, which have a higher content of potassium, are also available, but these should not be used by people with heart disease. If a salty meal has been eaten, several glasses of water should be drunk to lessen the strain on the kidneys.

Salt supplements are occasionally needed to prevent and treat the conditions of heat exhaustion and the more severe heat stroke, or heat hyperpyrexia. Heat exhaustion is collapse caused by overheating of the body and loss of fluid following unaccustomed or prolonged exposure to excessive temperatures. It is more common in hot climates and results from excessive sweating leading to loss of fluids and salts and disturbance of the electrolyte (mineral) balance in body fluids. In the mildest form, heat collapse, blood pressure and pulse rate fall, accompanied by fatigue, light-headedness and possibly muscular cramps. Treatment involves giving salt solutions, either by mouth or intravenously. Prevention is by means of gradual acclimatisation to the heat, especially if hard, physical work is to be carried out, and, possibly, salt tablets once the activity is undertaken. Heat stroke is a more severe condition in which there is a rapid rise in body temperature and sweating and regulatory mechanisms fail. There is a loss of consciousness, coma and death unless emergency treatment – involving cooling of the body and giving salt solutions, often intravenously – can be administered.

The RDA for sodium in the form of salt is 0.5–1.6g. Studies have shown that the average person in Western countries consumes at least twice this amount, and this is a contributory factor to high rates of the diseases mentioned above. Eating wholefoods and avoiding processed ones as much as possible is a good way of reducing sodium intake.

Potassium

Potassium is a vital component of cell and tissue fluids, helping to maintain the electrolyte/water balance, and is also essential for nerve function. The balance between potassium and sodium levels in the body may be quite significant in the development of some diseases and conditions. For example, low potassium/high sodium ratios are a factor in the development of hypertension (high blood pressure) and stress. Potassium levels are usually quite high in many wholefoods but are often reduced in highly processed ones. A deficiency in potassium causes appetite loss and sickness, bloating, weakness of muscles, increased thirst, a tingling sensation and pins and needles. Blood pressure falls, which may lead to light-headedness and, in severe cases, unconsciousness and coma. In general, sufficient potassium can be obtained from eating a normal, varied diet and the RDA is 1875–5625 mg. Enriched potassium supplements should not be taken by people suffering from heart disorders without first obtaining medical advice.

Calcium

Calcium is present in significant amounts in the human body, forming about two per cent of total mass and overwhelmingly concentrated in the bones and teeth. Calcium is vital for the growth and repair of the teeth and skeleton, and is particularly important for growing children, pregnant and postmenopausal women. The uptake and hence utilisation of calcium is controlled by vitamin D, but the mineral must first be broken down by stomach acid into a form that can be used. Hence, in the development and progression of some diseases, there may not be a straightforward relationship between dietary intake of calcium and what happens within the body. For example, patients with osteoporosis quite frequently have low levels of both stomach acid and the most potent form of vitamin D. Those suffering from Crohn's disease or irritable bowel syndrome may also go short of calcium as a result of deficiency of the vitamin, among other factors. Some people suffering from hypertension have been shown to have a lower than normal dietary intake of calcium.

Naturopaths may recommend calcium supplements for people suffering from certain medical conditions. The most useful form is as ionised, soluble calcium citrate, gluconate or lactate, as this is more readily absorbed than insoluble calcium carbonate. However, calcium carbonate is the usual form in which supplements are available. A deficiency of calcium, which is uncommon in those in good health who eat a normal varied diet, is rickets in children and osteomalacia in adults. Calcium-rich foods include milk and dairy

products, fish, flour, bread and fortified cereals. The RDA
is 500 mg.

Iron
Iron is an essential component of *haemoglobin*, the respiratory substance in red blood cells which picks up and transports oxygen from the lungs to all the body tissues. It consists of *haem*, a compound containing iron composed of a
pigment known as a porphyrin, which confers the red colour of the blood. This combines with the protein *globin* to
perform the vital task of transporting oxygen to, and removing carbon dioxide from, the tissues, which is then carried back to the lungs in the venous blood and eliminated.
Iron-rich foods include red meat, liver, kidney, egg yolk,
cocoa, nuts, green vegetables, such as spinach, dried figs,
apricots, raisins, pulses and fortified flour and cereals. Iron
is absorbed more readily from meat but its uptake is also
enhanced by plenty of vitamin C. A deficiency in iron causes
anaemia, with symptoms of tiredness, feeling cold, shortness of breath, dizziness and possible loss of appetite and
weight, swelling of the ankles and heartbeat irregularities.
Anaemia may also result from diseases or disorders of the
blood or other organs rather than an actual dietary lack of
iron. It is common in people suffering from leukaemia,
Crohn's disease or ulcerative colitis, in bleeding disorders,
in immune system disruption or in those who have suffered blood loss. Pregnant women and those who have just

given birth are also at risk of iron deficiency. The RDA is 800 mg.

Phosphorus

Phosphorus is present in the body in considerable amounts, making up about one per cent of total body weight and concentrated mainly in the bones and teeth. It is essential for the growth, health and maintenance of the teeth and skeleton, and the body's supply is totally renewed over two to three years. Phosphorus is also essential in energy metabolism and muscle activity, and in the function of some enzymes, and it also affects the absorption in the intestine of other elements and compounds. A deficiency in phosphorus is unlikely as it is widely found in foods but is present in particularly high concentrations in protein foods of animal origin. Symptoms of deficiency can include muscle and central nervous system disorders, weakness, malaise, anorexia and respiratory failure (in severe cases). An elevated intake of phosphorus, associated with a Western diet high in meat and dairy produce at the expense of plant foods, can reduce or prevent the absorption of iron, calcium, zinc and magnesium. This may be a factor in the incidence of osteoporosis and a number of other disorders. The RDA is 800 mg.

Magnesium

Magnesium is required for the growth, health and maintenance of bones and teeth, the correct functioning of nerves and muscles, and for metabolic processes involving certain enzymes. It is also involved in the functioning of vitamins B_1 and B_{12}. Magnesium is widely found in many foods, including green vegetables, cereals, whole grains, meat, milk and dairy products, eggs, shellfish, nuts and pulses. A deficiency causes anxiety, sleeplessness, trembling, palpitations, cramp-like muscle pains, sickness, and loss of appetite and weight. It may be a feature in premenstrual syndrome, low blood sugar (hypoglycaemia), angina pectoris, heart attack, Crohn's disease and ulcerative colitis, diabetes mellitus and retinopathy, hypertension, kidney stones and prolapse of the mitral valve in the heart, migraine and osteoporosis. Magnesium supplements may be helpful in the treatment of asthma, atherosclerosis, stress and alcoholism. The RDA is 300 mg.

Iodine
Iodine is vital for the correct functioning of the thyroid gland and is present in the hormones (thyroxine and triiodothyronine) that are essential for the regulation of metabolism and growth. Iodine is present in seaweed, seafoods and iodised salt, meat, vegetables and fruit grown on iodine-rich soils. A deficiency causes goitre, in which the thyroid gland enlarges in order to increase its output of hormones. There is a tiredness, lowered metabolism, weakness and weight gain. Iodine deficiency, combined with hypothyroidism, may be

associated with fibrocystic disease of the breasts and breast cancer, in some cases. The RDA is 140–150 micrograms (0.14–0.15 mg) but this amount is greatly exceeded in the average western diet. Iodine deficiency is now relatively rare because of the introduction of iodine into table salt.

Zinc

Zinc is essential for the functioning of numerous enzymes and is widely involved in metabolic processes. It is vital in vitamin A utilisation, is essential in immune system functioning, acts as an antioxidant and antiviral agent and ensures the healing of wounds. It is vital for insulin metabolism and hence the control of blood sugar. Deficiency has wide-ranging effects, including poor growth and development, including retardation of sexual and intellectual development, and slow wound healing. Zinc deficiency is common in people suffering from Crohn's disease, hypothyroidism and gum disease, and probably plays a part in susceptibility to viral infections and diabetes mellitus. It can be beneficial in the treatment of viral infections, including those of AIDS, prostate gland enlargement, rheumatoid arthritis, healing of wounds, alcoholism, acne, eczema and stress. The RDA is 15 mg.

Selenium

Selenium, in conjunction with vitamin E, is a powerful antioxidant and is particularly effective in counteracting the effects of toxic heavy metals such as mercury, lead and cadmium. Selenium is the co-factor necessary for the activity of the enzyme glutathione peroxidase, which mops up free radicals. The enzyme also reduces the formation of certain prostaglandins (hormone-like chemicals) that can cause inflammation and leukotrienes (compounds in white blood cells that are believed to be involved in allergic and inflammatory responses). It ensures correct functioning of the liver and blood system, but it is estimated that many people have a dietary deficiency of this mineral. Good sources of selenium include unrefined wholefoods, such as grains and cereals, egg yolks, kidney and liver, shellfish, garlic and yeast. Selenium supplements, along with vitamin E, can be beneficial in the treatment of various disorders, including cataracts, acne, psoriasis, alcoholism, skin cancer, cervical dysplasia (abnormal cells in the cervix), gum disease, rheumatoid arthritis and soft tissue injuries. A deficiency in selenium can cause effects on the heart and circulation, possible anaemia and may be a factor in sudden infant death syndrome (SIDS). The RDA is 0.05–0.2 mg.

Manganese
Manganese is essential for the activity of many enzymes and metabolic reactions. It is involved in nerve and muscle function, in growth and in the maintenance and health of the skeleton. It is a co-factor in a vital enzyme of glucose

metabolism, and some people suffering from diabetes mellitus have been shown to be deficient in manganese. Manganese is necessary for the activity of the enzyme superoxide dismutase, or manganese superoxide dismutase, which has antioxidant activity. This enzyme has been shown to be deficient in some people suffering from rheumatoid arthritis. Adequate intake of manganese may be helpful in preventing and treating this condition. Manganese is widely found in many foods but especially in whole grains, nuts, cereals, avocado pears, pulses and tea. A deficiency causes slow growth and bone abnormalities. The RDA is 2.5 mg, but an excess can be harmful, causing learning disabilities and central nervous system effects.

Copper
Copper is involved in the activity of many enzymes and metabolic functions. It is necessary for the growth and maintenance of bones and is involved in the production of red blood cells. It is involved in the production of connective tissue and in the metabolism of fats, and deficiency may be a factor in the development of atherosclerosis and osteoarthritis. The zinc-copper balance has been shown to be important in the development of some conditions as the two minerals may 'compete' with one another to a certain extent. A deficiency in copper is normally uncommon but can cause reduced number of white blood cells, hence lowered immunity, and changes in the hair. The wearing of cop-

per bracelets can be beneficial in the treatment of rheumatoid arthritis. However, excessive intake of copper can be harmful and may be involved in causing joint damage and learning difficulties and in increased susceptibility to gum disease. The RDA is 0.05–0.2 mg.

Chromium
Chromium is important in a range of metabolic activities, particularly the utilisation and storage of sugars and fats. It is involved in the activity of insulin, in glucose tolerance in diabetes and in immune system function. Chromium is essential for the correct functioning of the voluntary muscles that move the bones and joints. Chromium is found in whole and unrefined foods, including wholemeal flour, whole grains, cereals, brewer's yeast, nuts, meat, liver, kidney and fresh fruits. A deficiency may cause irritability and depression, forgetfulness and sleep disturbances. Chromium can be helpful in the treatment of acne, atherosclerosis and diabetes mellitus. The RDA is 0.05–0.2 mg.

Sulphur
Sulphur is involved in amino acid metabolism and manufacture of proteins and hence is important in the structural components of the body – bones, teeth, nails and skin. Sulphur-containing amino acids (proteins) called methionine and cysteine are possibly involved in human longevity and tend to decline in older age. Good dietary sources are eggs,

meat, liver, pulses, garlic, onions, nuts, brewer's yeast, fish and dairy products. Deficiency is not reported and there is no RDA.

Strontium

Strontium is similar in composition to calcium and, like that mineral, is naturally found concentrated in bones and teeth. There has been justifiable fear about strontium 90, a product of nuclear fallout that can enter the food chain and become concentrated in the human body. However, non-radioactive strontium, obtained from foods such as milk and other dairy produce, helps to ensure the strength of bone and can be beneficial in the treatment of osteoporosis. The RDA is not known.

Boron

Boron is thought to be involved, as a trace element, in the utilisation of calcium and in the activity of vitamin D and the hormone oestrogen. It is thought to be necessary for the conversion of vitamin D into its most potent, active form, 1_1 25–dihydroxyvitamin D_3, which takes place in the kidney. Boron is found especially in fresh vegetables and fruits, and can be beneficial in the treatment of osteoporosis in postmenopausal women. High concentrations of the mineral are, however, toxic, and there is no RDA.

Free radicals and antioxidants

Free radicals are naturally occurring, unstable compounds that are very reactive. They have an additional proton or electron within their structure, which allows them to freely attach to, and destroy, useful molecules. The majority of free radicals are produced within the body, and among the most potent are toxic oxygen molecules. These are able to oxidise useful substances within the body, which is harmful. Substances that are able to counteract or prevent this damage are termed *antioxidants*. The body produces several known antioxidant enzymes, including glutathione peroxidase and superoxide dismutase, and some vitamins and minerals are also active in this way. External sources of free radicals include tobacco smoke, chemicals (paints, solvents, petroleum-based products, glues, some cleaning fluids and DIY substances), exhaust emissions, alcohol, radiation, agricultural chemicals and fertilisers, and sunlight. Environmental sources of free radicals should be avoided as far as possible, particularly those that are under an individual's direct control, such as smoking or drinking too much alcohol or coffee. One cannot entirely prevent the formation of free radicals within the body, but it is possible to make sure that the diet contains plenty of antioxidant substances. Vitamins and minerals that have important antioxidant activity include Vitamins C and E, selenium and sulphur. Two other groups of plant substances have also been found to be very important: carotenes and flavonoids.

Carotenes

Carotenes are hydrocarbon molecules containing carotenoids – orange, yellow or red pigments that are found quite widely among plants and in some animal tissues (egg yolk, milk, fat). About 40 to 50 of known carotenoids can be converted into vitamin A within the body and are precursors of provitamin A. However, many of the carotenes studied (of which the best known is beta-carotene) have been demonstrated to have potent antioxidant activity. Carotenes are naturally deposited in body tissues and in the thymus gland, which functions in the immune system. There is now a growing body of evidence suggesting that the concentration of carotenes within the body, along with naturally occurring antioxidant enzymes, are factors determining the length of the lifespan in mammals, including human beings. It is postulated that the assault and destruction of cellular material, including DNA, is a significant factor in the ageing process.

In youth, the body is believed to be better able to repair the damage through the activity of naturally occurring protective mechanisms such as antioxidant enzymes. However, it is thought that the damaging effects are cumulative and that the body's repair mechanisms are not able to keep up, so that ageing and death eventually take place. In addition, it is believed that increased free radical damage favours the development of certain diseases, such as cancer, and also some of the conditions associated with ageing. It has been demonstrated that eating a diet rich in carotenes raises the level of these nutrients in the tissues, hence increasing anti-oxidant availability. The best sources are carrots, green leafy vegetables, including spinach and broccoli, beets, sweet potatoes (yams) and others. A good intake of carotenes helps to protect the body against certain forms of cancer, particularly of the digestive and respiratory systems, including the lungs, skin and cervix (neck of the womb). Also, immune system functions, mediated by the thymus gland, may be supported by a good dietary intake of carotenes. These include the vital production of T-lymphocyte white blood cells which produce antibodies that combat infection.

Flavonoids
Flavonoids are a group of naturally occurring plant pigments that are widely found in fruits (particularly berries such as blackberries, cherries, bilberries, blackcurrants, etc), vegetables and flowers. In addition to having antioxidant activity and the ability to 'mop up' free radicals, they also appear to have anti-carcinogenic, antiviral, anti-allergy and anti-inflammatory properties. It has also been discovered that certain flavonoids apparently possess specific affinity for particular tissues. Several thousand flavonoids have been identified and studied, particularly those from plants and herbs that have a long history of traditional medicinal use. In many cases, the interesting fact has emerged that plants that have been used for particular medicinal purposes do

indeed demonstrate specific flavonoid activity for the particular tissues or organs involved. In naturopathy, the use of particular plants or their extracts for their flavonoid activity may be recommended in the treatment of various diseases and conditions. A good intake of flavonoids can be ensured by eating a diet rich in fruit and vegetables.

Water

The human body is largely composed of water, and it is essential to all life processes. Naturopaths recommend that at least six to eight glasses of plain water should be drunk each day, particularly to ensure the correct functioning of the kidneys and digestive system. More water is needed during hot weather to compensate for the natural loss through sweating. Also, drinking plain water (preferably as frequent, small sips) is very important for people suffering from a bout of diarrhoea or vomiting. In naturopathy, water plays an important part in detoxification and also in hydrotherapy.

Detoxification

The human body is continuously exposed to harmful or even poisonous substances in the course of day-to-day life. Some of these are produced within the body itself as the waste products of essential metabolic processes. Examples are urea and ammonia, produced as a result of protein metabolism, and carbon dioxide, which is the waste product of tissue respiration. Also, bacteria, notably those in the gut, produce toxins that can be absorbed into the body and produce harm. In addition, there are an enormous number of harmful substances in the environment to which the human body is inevitably exposed. These may be eaten in food, drunk in water, absorbed through the skin or breathed in from the air. The range of substances is enormous but includes heavy metals such as lead, mercury, arsenic, cadmium, industrial chemicals and solvents, cleaning fluids, pesticides, glues, drugs, alcohol, smoke and toxins produced by harmful, infective bacteria. The body has its own organs and systems to protect itself against, and to deal with, this constant barrage of harmful substances. The major organ involved is the liver but also the kidneys, lungs, digestive tract and immune system. A person's health and the prevention of disease are very much dependent upon the effectiveness of the body's detoxification mechanisms.

Naturopaths may recommend a specific programme of detoxification, either to help eliminate a particular toxin or for the promotion of general health. A buildup of a toxic substance can produce a variety of symptoms, depending upon the nature of the material involved. Symptoms include neurological disturbances, tremor, headaches, digestive upset, pains, tiredness, anaemia, loss of coordination and depression. A number of diagnostic tests may be performed to detect the presence of toxic poisoning. These include the analysis of hair (especially for heavy metals), examination of urine or stool samples, and serum bile assay. These must be carried out in specialist laboratories, usually when there is reason to suspect the presence of a particular toxic substance. It is believed that heavy metal poisoning is a more common problem than is generally realised.

Detoxification programmes

The most commonly recommended method in naturopathy is controlled *fasting*, which is the stopping of all eating and drinking (except for pure water) for a specific period of time. Before a fast is undertaken, a thorough medical examination is needed to ensure that the person is fit enough for the process. The benefits of fasting are that it enables the body to 'rest' from its usual metabolic activities and to eliminate stored toxic substances. Fat reserves are used to supply energy needs during the process. Fasting is certainly a very ancient remedy, known to have been used by many different peoples throughout the world. Plenty of rest is essential during a fast so that the body is not unduly stressed. Stored toxic substances are removed from the tissues during a fast and enter the bloodstream so that they can be dealt with by the organs of detoxification. This begins to happen quite soon after the commencement of a fast, and may cause early unpleasant symptoms such as headaches, bad breath and diarrhoea, which, however, quickly pass.

In the case of some chemical poisons, such as the pesticide DDT, which are stored in body fat, fasting may cause the blood level to rise to a degree that is harmful to the nervous system. Hence a fast must always be undertaken carefully in the case of known poisons.

In addition to general detoxification, fasting may help in the relief of certain medical conditions, including hypertension (high blood pressure), arthritis, rheumatism, skin conditions, food allergies and digestive disorders. It is, of course, well known that going without food for a period of 24 hours is helpful in getting over a bout of diarrhoea and vomiting, by enabling the digestive system to rest and eliminate the causative bacteria. A short fast usually lasts for three to five days and, after an initial medical check-up, can usually be undertaken at home. During the fast, naturopaths recommend no contact with any synthetic chemicals such as might be contained in household cleaners, detergents, cosmetics, deodorants and perfumes. Hard exercise should be avoided, baths or showers should be with lukewarm water, and plenty of rest is beneficial. Extra clothing and warm surroundings are needed as, during the fast, body temperature is lowered and the metabolic rate slows down. Longer periods of fasting are usually undertaken at a health clinic or sanatorium so that the condition of the person can be closely monitored. Various supplements may be recommended, such as vitamin C, goldenseal root and silymarin, to enhance and support the process of detoxification.

Care must be taken when breaking a fast, and it is important to make sure that small quantities are eaten at first. Naturopaths may recommend breaking a fast with a piece of fruit or some salad, either of which can be eaten for the first day or two. The wholefoods that are normally eaten can then be gradually reintroduced. A healthy, wholefood diet promotes continual natural detoxification in which occasional periods of fasting may prove beneficial as a booster.

Recognising, Understanding and Managing Stress

Stress can be defined as a state of physical and mental tension caused by certain external or internal factors in a person's life. The causes of stress are varied and numerous, and so are people's responses to them. The cause may be something obvious, which would produce symptoms of stress in almost anyone, such as extreme physical danger with the expectation of imminent death or disaster. Or it may be a far more subtle, mental anxiety that causes extreme stress in one individual but may be a matter of complete indifference in another. Stress is a part of the human condition, maintaining alertness for life, and, to some extent, is unavoidable. Human beings and other mammals possess physiological adaptations, which almost certainly evolved as a survival aid, equipping them to deal more effectively with external physical dangers and stresses. These adaptations are based on the release of hormones from the adrenal glands and the nerve endings of the sympathetic nervous system, namely, adrenaline, noradrenaline, cortisol and cortisone. These hormones prepare the body for 'fright, flight or fight' by increasing the depth and rate of respiration, raising the heartbeat and increasing muscle performance as a result of an improved blood supply and elevation in the level of available glucose. In addition, the pupils dilate and distance vision is enhanced, blood vessels constrict, release of saliva decreases, sweating and blood pressure increase, and the processes of digestion and excretion are inhibited. The body and mind are prepared and tense, ready for immediate activity, and the physical manifestations subside once avoiding action has been taken or the danger has passed.

People react in a similar way to emotional and psychological stress but in these cases, the physiological adaptations are not only unhelpful but can be damaging, especially if prolonged. An example of short-term emotional stress is being on the receiving end of unwarranted, unpleasant verbal remarks, particularly if it does not seem possible to defend oneself. More prolonged emotional or psychological stress can be caused, for example, by a difficult relationship, the illness and suffering of a loved one or the continual pressure posed by too great a workload. Many people are victims of both short-term and long-term emotional and psychological stress. Stress causes both physical and mental symptoms, some of which are more obvious than others, so that a person is not necessarily aware that he or she is experiencing the effects of this condition. This is because of the fact that the mind and body adapt to the stressed state so that the signs and symptoms can go unrecognised. Symptoms that frequently occur include:

- panic attacks and breathing difficulties
- palpitations
- anxiety
- insomnia
- irritability, impatience, angry outbursts
- pains almost anywhere, particularly digestive and abdominal
- tense muscles causing aches and pains
- frequent headaches
- increased reliance on alcohol, smoking, coffee, etc.
- tiredness, lack of concentration, indecision

In recognising the causes of stress, it can be helpful to look carefully at each aspect of life, i.e. home and family, work and other relationships, and to make some honest assessments, perhaps with the help of a partner. Also, during the course of a normal week, make a note of the times and occasions when symptoms of stress arise as this is likely to help to identify the exact cause. It is then necessary to deal with these problems, beginning with those that are most significant. Initially, many people feel that this is impossible, particularly if the problems relate to work, and especially in the current climate of insecurity relating to employment.

However, taking charge of the problems and, above all, discussing things frankly with work colleagues, are vital steps in managing stress. Most firms would prefer to find solutions for problems rather than have an employee taking lots of time off work because of stress-related illness. Likewise, if the causes of stress relate to home or some other aspect of life, it is important to bring these out into the open and to discuss them with those concerned. Usually, this brings a great sense of relief and immediate lessening of stress. Also, depending upon the nature of the problem, there may be professional organisations or self-help groups that are able to offer support and advice. Many people believe that they should be able to deal with problems themselves and have associated feelings of guilt and failure when they are unable to cope. Another common feeling is the belief that the person undergoing the stress is the only person experiencing problems and that others are managing well and would not understand what he or she is going through. In fact, once problems start to be discussed, a person is usually surprised to realise how many others have had similar experiences. Usually, this too can bring an enormous sense of relief.

Once the process of identifying and dealing with the causes of stress is initiated, there are other measures that can help. Firstly, a person needs to recognise that health and wellbeing matter not only to himself or herself but also to family and friends. Time should therefore be made in the weekly routine to allow space for hobbies, recreational and social activities that will divert attention away from problems. It is important to take plenty of exercise, as this encourages restful sleep, which is, in itself, an important part of stress management. Also, it is helpful to learn and practise a relaxation routine, which usually involves simple exercises, breathing patterns and possibly meditation and visualisation therapy. There are many books available on this subject, and yoga is one well-known example of this technique. Some alternative therapies, such as aromatherapy and massage, are very helpful in relieving muscular stress and tension. Regular exercise is also of great importance.

Prolonged stress is a serious condition that is known to increase the risk of developing certain illnesses, some of which are life-threatening. These include hypertension, stroke, angina, heart attack, circulatory disorders, ulcers, headaches, depression, mental breakdown, irritable bowel syndrome and immune system depression, which increases the likelihood of some infections. The adrenal glands are vitally important in the body's ability to cope with stress through their secretion of hormones that are involved in producing the 'fright, flight or fight' reaction. Also involved are two other groups of hormones. The glucocorticosteroids and mineralocorticosteroids are produced by the adrenal cortex and are involved in energy metabolism and regulation of the electrolytes/water balance within the body. Prolonged stress can cause the adrenal glands to work less effectively and places strain on the heart and circulation and immune system. Vital potassium stores tend to become depleted, affecting the function of all tissue cells. Hence, in the management of stress, naturopaths are likely to recommend a diet rich in potassium-containing foods and other nutrients that enhance the function of the adrenal glands. These include vitamins C and B$_6$, pantothenic acid, magnesium and zinc. Among the plant extracts, ginseng is particularly beneficial in helping the body to deal with stress and to promote the activity of the adrenal glands. Other herbal teas and soothing preparations may be recommended as a useful aid to relaxation.

Herbal Remedies

Herbalism is sometimes maligned as a collection of home-made remedies to be applied in a placebo fashion to one symptom or another, provided the ailment is not too serious and provided there is a powerful chemical wonder-drug at the ready to suppress any 'real' symptoms. We often forget, however, that botanical medicine provides a complete system of healing and disease prevention. It is the oldest and most natural form of medicine. Its record of efficacy and safety spans centuries and covers every country in the world. Because herbal medicine is holistic medicine, it is, in fact, able to look beyond the symptoms to the underlying systemic imbalance. When skilfully applied by a trained practitioner, herbal medicine offers very real and permanent solutions to concrete problems, many of them seemingly intractable to pharmaceutical intervention.

Early civilisations

The medicinal use of herbs is said to be as old as mankind itself. In early civilisations, food and medicine were linked and many plants were eaten for their health-giving properties. In ancient Egypt, the slave workers were given a daily ration of garlic to help fight off the many fevers and infections that were common at that time. The first written records of herbs and their beneficial properties were compiled by the ancient Egyptians. Most of our knowledge and use of herbs can be traced back to the Egyptian priests who also practised herbal medicine. Records dating back to 1500 BC listed medicinal herbs, including caraway and cinnamon. The ancient Greeks and Romans also carried out herbal medicine, and as they invaded new lands, their doctors encountered new herbs and introduced herbs such as rosemary or lavender into new areas. Other cultures with a history of herbal medicine are those of the Chinese and the Indians. In Britain, the use of herbs developed along with the establishment of monasteries around the country, each of which had its own herb garden for use in treating both the monks and the local people. In some areas, particularly in Wales and Scotland, druids and other Celtic healers are thought to have had an oral tradition of herbalism, in which medicine was mixed with religion and ritual.

Over time, these healers and their knowledge led to the writing of the first 'herbals', books that described the properties of plants, which rapidly rose in importance and distribution upon the advent of the printing press in the 15th century. John Parkinson of London wrote a herbal around 1630, listing useful plants. Many herbalists set up their own apothecary shops, including the famous Nicholas Culpepper (1616–54) whose most famous work is *The Complete Herbal and Physician, Enlarged*, published in 1649. Then in 1812, Henry Potter started a business supplying herbs and dealing in leeches. By this time a huge amount of traditional knowledge and folklore on medicinal herbs was available from Britain, Europe, the Middle East, Asia and the Americas. This promoted Potter to write *Potter's Encyclopaedia of Botanical Drugs and Preparations*, which is still published today.

It was in this period that scientifically inspired conventional medicine rose in popularity, sending herbal medicine into a decline. In rural areas, herbal medicine continued to thrive in local folklore, traditions and practices. In 1864 the National Association (later Institute) of Medical Herbalists was established to organise the training of herbal medicine practitioners and to maintain standards of practice. From 1864 until the early part of the 20th century, the Institute fought attempts to ban herbal medicine, and over time public interest in herbal medicine has increased, particularly over the last 20 years of the 20th century. This move away from synthetic drugs is partly because of possible side effects, bad publicity, and, in some instances, a mistrust of the medical and pharmacological industries. The more natural appearance of herbal remedies has led to its growing support and popularity. Herbs from America have been incorporated with common remedies, and scientific research into herbs and their active ingredients has confirmed their healing power and enlarged the range of medicinal herbs used today.

Herbal medicine can be viewed as the precursor of modern pharmacology, but today it continues as an effective and more natural method of treating and preventing illness. Globally, herbal medicine is three to four times more commonly practised than conventional medicine. Nowhere is the efficacy of herbalism more evident than in problems related to the nervous system. Stress, anxiety, tension and depression are intimately connected with most illness. Few health practitioners would argue with the influence of nervous anxiety in pathology. Nervous tension is generally acknowledged by doctors to contribute to duodenal and gastric ulceration, ulcerative colitis, irritable bowel syndrome and many other gut-related pathologies.

We know also, from physiology, that when a person is depressed, the secretion of hydrochloric acid – one of the main digestive juices – is also reduced, so that digestion and absorption are rendered less efficient. Anxiety, on the other hand, can lead to the release of adrenaline and stimulate the overproduction of hydrochloric acid and result in a state of acidity that may exacerbate the pain of an inflamed ulcer. In fact, whenever the voluntary nervous system (our conscious anxiety) interferes with the autonomic processes (the automatic nervous regulation that in health is never made conscious), illness is the result.

Herbalists rely on their knowledge of botanical remedies to rectify this type of human malfunction. The medical herbalist will treat a stubborn dermatological problem using 'alternatives' specific to the skin problem, and then apply circulatory stimulants to aid in the removal of toxins from the area, with remedies to reinforce other organs of elimination, such as the liver and kidneys. Under such natural treatment, free from any discomforting side effects, the patient can feel confident and relaxed – perhaps for the first time in many months. Curiously, this is an approach that has never been taken up by orthodox medicine. There, the usual treatment of skin problems involves suppression of symptoms with steroids. However, the use of conventional antihistamines or benzodiazepines often achieves less lasting benefit to the patient because of the additional burden of side effects such as drowsiness, increased toxicity, and long-term drug dependence.

Because they are organic substances and not synthetic molecules, herbs possess an affinity for the human organism. They are extremely efficient in balancing the nervous system. Restoring a sense of wellbeing and relaxation is necessary for optimum health and for the process of self-healing. Naturally, the choice of a treatment should be based upon a thorough health assessment and the experience and training of a qualified herbal practitioner. The herbalist will then prepare and prescribe herbal remedies in a variety of different forms, such as infusions, loose teas, suppositories, inhalants, lotions, tinctures, tablets and pills. Many of these preparations are available for home use from chemists, health shops and mail-order suppliers.

Herbs for stress management

Chamomile
This has a relaxing effect on the mind and body. It is an excellent sedative for anxiety and muscle tenseness. Many people enjoy its benefits in the form of chamomile tea.

Valerian
This is the ideal tranquilliser. The rhizomes of this plant contain a volatile oil (which includes valerianic acid), volatile alkaloids (including chatinine) and iridoids (valepotriates), which have been shown to reduce anxiety and aggression. So effective is valerian in relieving anxiety while maintaining normal mental awareness that it enables us to continue the most complicated mental exercise without drowsiness, loss of consciousness or depression. Valerian has been usefully taken before an examination or a driving test!

Peppermint
This is effective for treating digestive discomfort: it relieves indigestion, flatulence, constipation and nausea. Peppermint is also a good mind tonic, helping to clarify ideas and focus concentration. It is also helpful in alleviating the symptoms of colds and influenza. Peppermint and chamomile tea is thought to be effective in reducing the pain of tension headaches and migraines.

St John's wort
Also called *Hypericum perforatum*, St John's wort has an-

algesic and anti-inflammatory properties, with important local applications to neuralgia and sciatica. Systemically, its sedative properties are based on the glycoside hypericin (a red pigment), which makes it applicable to neurosis and irritability. Many herbalists use it extensively as a background remedy.

Lemon balm
This herb is both carminative and antispasmodic, and is active specifically on that part of the vagus nerve that may interfere with the harmonious functioning of the heart and the stomach. Recent research has indicated that the action of the volatile oil begins within the limbic system of the brain and subsequently operates directly upon the vagus nerve and all the organs that are innervated by it. Accordingly, neurasthenia (complete nervous prostration), migraine and nervous gastropathy are amenable to its healing power.

Lime flowers
These are thought to be helpful in controlling anxiety and hyperactivity. They are also effective for treating insomnia, high blood pressure and for soothing muscles and nerves.

Borage
This is an effective mind tonic, which helps to alleviate headaches, migraine and depression.

Oats
This is one of the great herbal restoratives of the nervous

system. The plant contains a nervine alkaloid that is helpful in angina and in cardiac insufficiency. It has also been used in the treatment of addiction to morphine, narcotics, tobacco and alcohol.

Soothing herbal drinks

Warm milk and honey
Perhaps with a dash of cinnamon, this is an ideal drink to take at bedtime. It will help you relax and ward off insomnia.

Hop tea
Three hop cones, or heads, infused in a cup of boiling water whenever you begin to feel excessively tense, is a marvellous remedy for anxiety and insomnia.

A soothing herb tea to sustain a feeling of equilibrium
　　25g (1 oz) each dried chamomile flowers, lime flowers,
　　　　hibiscus blossoms and marigold flowers
　　15g ($^1/_2$ oz) each dried peppermint leaves and vervain
　　1 teaspoon whole fenugreek seeds
　　100g (4 oz) Lapsang Souchong tea
Mix all the ingredients together and store in a dark airtight container. Use 1 teaspoon to 300 ml ($^1/_2$ pint) of boiling water in a teapot and leave to infuse for five minutes before straining and serving with a slice of lemon and a teaspoon of honey if desired. This is a very calming tea that soothes feelings of anxiety. It also helps to clear the head and settle

an upset tummy. One cup taken morning and night will promote a feeling of wellbeing.

Another calming tea, especially good for the nerves

1 teaspoon each grated valerian root and dried mint

$^1/_2$ teaspoon each dried chamomile and lavender flowers

600 ml (1 pint) boiling water

Infuse the dry ingredients in the water for 15 minutes then strain and take a glass three times a day for one week only.

Two tonic teas to sip when feeling depressed

Sip either 2 teaspoons of dandelion and 1 of basil infused in 600 ml (1 pint) of boiling water, or 2 teaspoons each of nettle, basil and melissa infused in 600 ml (1 pint) of boiling water.

A tonic tea to relieve stress and anxiety

1 tablespoon each fresh dandelion and nettle tops

1 teaspoon each fresh blackcurrant and borage leaves

600 ml (1 pint) boiling water

Steep the greenery in the water for five minutes. Strain and drink with lemon and honey.

Dock wine

Dock is one of the great tonic herbs because it is extremely high in iron. Here is a recipe for an old-fashioned dock wine:

175g (7 oz) dock root

15g ($^1/_2$ oz) liquorice wood

7g ($^{1}/_{4}$ oz) juniper berries

100g (4 oz) raw cane sugar

2 litres ($3^{1}/_{2}$ pints) organic red wine

Put the ingredients in a china container, cover and place either in a very slow oven or in a bain marie. Continue to heat gently until the mixture is reduced by half. Strain, bottle and seal tightly. Drink a sherry glass of the wine every morning for two weeks.

Rosemary in wine

Steep 6 sprigs of rosemary in a well-sealed bottle of sweet white wine for 14 days. Take 1 wine glass as a daily tonic.

Sage tonic

Take 100g (4 oz) of fresh sage leaves and put them in a bottle of organic white wine for two weeks. Sweeten to taste with honey and leave for another day. Press and strain through muslin. Bottle, and take 1 sherry glass before lunch and dinner.

You can also infuse sage leaves in boiling water, strain and sweeten with honey for an uplifting sage tea.

Examples of herbs

Agrimony *Agrimonia eupatoria*.

COMMON NAME: church steeples, cockleburr, sticklewort.

OCCURRENCE: field borders, ditches and hedges throughout England. Found locally in Scotland.

PARTS USED: the herb, which contains a particular volatile oil, tannin and a bitter principle.

MEDICINAL USES: mild astringent, tonic, diuretic, deobstruent. It has a reputation for curing liver complaints and is very good for skin eruptions and blood diseases. It is also recommended to treat the sting and bite of snakes.

ADMINISTERED AS: liquid extract.

Allspice *Pimento officinalis*.

COMMON NAME: pimento, Jamaica pepper, clove pepper.

OCCURRENCE: indigenous to the West Indies and South America; cultivated in Jamaica and Central America.

PARTS USED: the fruit, which contains a volatile oil made up of eugenol, a sesquiterpene and other unknown chemicals.

MEDICINAL USES: aromatic, stimulant, carminative. Allspice acts on the gastrointestinal tract and is usually added to drinks tonics and purgatives for flavouring. The spice may also be used for flatulent indigestion and hysteria. Allspice is frequently used as a spice and condiment in food or drinks.

ADMINISTERED AS: essential oil, distilled water, powdered fruit, fluid extract.

Aloes *Aloe perryi, Aloe vera*.

OCCURRENCE: indigenous to East and South Africa and introduced into the West Indies.

PARTS USED: the drug aloes is described as 'the liquid evaporated to dryness, which drains from the leaves.' It contains two aloin compounds, barbaloin and isobarbaloin, as well as amorphous aloin, resin and aloe-emodin in differing proportions.

MEDICINAL USES: emmenagogue, purgative, vermifuge, anthelmintic. It is generally administered along with carminative and anodyne drugs, and acts on the lower bowel. The liquid form may be used externally to ease skin irritation.

ADMINISTERED AS: fluid extract, powdered extract, decoction, tincture.

Anemone, Pulsatilla *Anemone pulsatilla*.

COMMON NAME: pasqueflower, meadow anemone, wind flower.

OCCURRENCE: found locally in chalk downs and limestone areas of England.

PARTS USED: the whole herb. It produces oil of anemone upon distillation with water.

MEDICINAL USES: nervine, antispasmodic, alterative and diaphoretic. It is beneficial in disorders of mucous membranes and of the respiratory and digestive passages. Can be used to treat asthma, whooping cough and bronchitis.

ADMINISTERED AS: fluid extract.

Anemone, Wood *Anemone nemorosa*.

COMMON NAME: crowfoot, windflower, smell fox.

OCCURRENCE: found in woods and thickets across Great Britain.

PARTS USED: the root, leaves and juice.

MEDICINAL USES: this species of plant is much less widely used than it has been previously. It used to be good for leprosy, lethargy, eye inflammation and headaches. An ointment made of the leaves is said to be effective in cleansing malignant ulcers.

ADMINISTERED AS: decoction, fresh leaves and root, ointment.

Angelica *Angelica archangelica*.

COMMON NAME: garden angelica, *Archangelica officinalis*.

OCCURRENCE: found native to some sites in Scotland, abundant in Lapland and is a common garden plant in England.

PARTS USED: the root, leaves and seeds. The leaves contain volatile oil, valeric acid, angelic acid, a bitter principle and a resin called angelicin. The roots contain terebangelene and other terpenes while the seeds also yield two acid compounds.

MEDICINAL USES: Angelica has carminative, stimulant, diaphoretic, diuretic, aromatic, stomachic, tonic and expectorant properties and is good for colds, coughs, pleurisy, wind, colic and rheumatism. It is used as a stimulating expectorant and is good for digestion.

ADMINISTERED AS: powdered root, liquid extract, infusion or as a poultice.

Angostura *Galipea officinalis*.

COMMON NAME: cusparia bark, *Cusparia febrifuga*, *Bonplandia trifoliata*, *Galipea cusparia*.

OCCURRENCE: a small tree native to tropical South America.
PARTS USED: the dried bark, which has the active ingredients angosturin, the alkaloids galipine, cusparine, galipidine, cusparidine and cuspareine, as well as a volatile oil and an unidentified glucoside.
MEDICINAL USES: aromatic, bitter, tonic, stimulant, purgative. There is a long history of usage by native South Americans as a stimulant tonic. It is useful in bilious diarrhoea and dysentery, but in large doses it has a purgative and cathartic effect on the body.
ADMINISTERED AS: infusion, powdered bark, tincture, fluid extract.

Anise *Pimpinella anisum*.
COMMON NAME: aniseed.
OCCURRENCE: native to Egypt, Greece, Crete and western Asia, its cultivation spread to central Europe and North Africa.
PARTS USED: the fruit. Upon distillation, the fruit yields a fragrant volatile oil that is made up of anethol, choline, a fixed oil, sugar and mucilage.
MEDICINAL USES: carminative and pectoral. It is very useful against coughs and chest infections and is made into lozenges or smoked to clear the chest. Aniseed tea is good for infant catarrh, and aids digestion in adults. Anise seed is an ingredient of cathartic and aperient pills, to relieve flatulence and lessen the griping caused by purgative herbs. It can also be given in convulsions quite safely.

ADMINISTERED AS: essence, essential oil, tincture, powdered seeds, tea and pills.

Arrowroot *Maranta arundinacea.*

COMMON NAME: *Maranta indica*, *M. ramosissima*, maranta starch or arrowroot, araruta, Bermuda arrowroot, Indian arrowroot.

OCCURRENCE: indigenous to the West Indies and central America. It is cultivated in Bengal, Java, the Philippines, Mauritius and West Africa.

PARTS USED: the dried, powdered starch from the rhizome.

MEDICINAL USES: nutritive, demulcent, non-irritating. Well suited for infants and convalescents, particularly after bowel complaints. The jelly made of water or milk may be flavoured with sugar, lemon juice or fruit. The fresh rhizomes are mashed and applied to wounds from poisoned arrows, scorpion or spider bites and to stop gangrene. The freshly expressed juice of the rhizome, when mixed with water, is said to be a good antidote against vegetable poisons.

ADMINISTERED AS: fresh root, expressed juice, dietary item.

Balm *Melissa officinalis.*

COMMON NAME: sweet balm, lemon balm, honey plant, cure-all.

OCCURRENCE: a common garden plant in Great Britain, which was naturalised into southern England at a very early period.

PARTS USED: the herb.

MEDICINAL USES: as a carminative, diaphoretic, or febrifuge.

It can be made into a cooling tea for fever patients and balm is often used in combination with other herbs to treat colds and fever.

ADMINISTERED AS: an infusion.

Barley *Hordeum distichon* and *Hordeum vulgare*.
COMMON NAME: pearl barley, *Perlatum*.
OCCURRENCE: throughout Britain.
PARTS USED: decorticated seeds, composed of eighty per cent starch and six per cent proteins, cellulose, etc.
MEDICINAL USES: barley is used to prepare a nutritive and demulcent drink for ill and fevered patients. Barley water is given to sick children suffering from diarrhoea or bowel inflammation, etc. Malt extract is also used medicinally.
ADMINISTERED AS: an infusion and beverage.

Basil *Ocimum basilicum*.
COMMON NAME: sweet basil, garden basil.
OCCURRENCE: as a garden plant throughout Britain.
PARTS USED: the herb, which contains a volatile, camphoraceous oil.
MEDICINAL USES: aromatic with carminative and cooling properties. It is used to treat mild nervous disorders, and an infusion of basil is said to be good for obstructions of the internal organs and in stopping vomiting and nausea.
ADMINISTERED AS: a flavouring in food, dried leaves or an infusion.

Belladonna *Atropa belladonna*.

COMMON NAME: deadly nightshade, devil's cherries, dwale, black cherry, devil's herb, great morel.

OCCURRENCE: native to central and southern Europe but commonly grows in England.

PARTS USED: the roots and leaves. The root contains several alkaloid compounds, including hyoscyamine, atropine and belladonnine. The same alkaloids are present in the leaves but the amount of each compound varies according to plant type and methods of storing and drying leaves.

MEDICINAL USES: as a narcotic, diuretic, sedative, mydriatic, antispasmodic. The drug is used as an anodyne in febrile conditions, night sweats and coughs. It is valuable in treating eye diseases and is used as a pain-relieving lotion to treat neuralgia, gout, rheumatism and sciatica. Belladonna is an extremely poisonous plant and should always be used under medical supervision – cases of accidental poisoning and death are well known. Despite this, it is a valuable drug used to treat a wide range of disease.

ADMINISTERED AS: a liquid extract that is used to produce alcoholic extracts, plasters, liniment, suppositories, tincture and ointment.

Bergamot *Monarda didyma*.

COMMON NAME: scarlet monarda, Oswego tea, bee balm.

OCCURRENCE: a plant that is indigenous to North America.

PARTS USED: the oil extracted from the whole plant, and the leaves.

MEDICINAL USES: used in a similar manner to other plants containing thymol as an active chemical. Oil of bergamot has antiseptic, aromatic, carminative, tonic and antispasmodic properties. An infusion of the young leaves was a common beverage in the USA before tea became more common. The infusion is also good for coughs, sore throats, fevers and colds.

ADMINISTERED AS: essential oil, infusion, fluid extract.

Bluebell *Scilla nutans, Hyacinthus nonscriptus.*
COMMON NAME: calverkeys, culverkeys, auld man's bell, ring o' bells, jacinth, wood bells, *Agraphis nutans.*
OCCURRENCE: abundant in western Europe, Great Britain and Italy.
PARTS USED: the bulb, dried and powdered.
MEDICINAL USES: diuretic, styptic. This medicine is little used today but it was considered a very powerful remedy for leucorrhoea. It may also have been used to cure snake bite. The fresh bulbs are poisonous, so the plant is always used when dried.
ADMINISTERED AS: powdered bulb.

Borage *Borago officinalis.*
COMMON NAME: burrage.
OCCURRENCE: naturalised in Britain and Europe and is found in gardens, rubbish heaps and near houses.
PARTS USED: the leaves and flowers consist of potassium, calcium and mineral acids along with nitrogen salts.

MEDICINAL USES: diuretic, demulcent, emollient, refrigerant.
It is effective in treating fevers and pulmonary complaints
as it activates the kidneys. It is applied externally as a
poultice against inflammation and swelling and has been
developed into a cream that treats itch and skin complaints,
e.g. eczema and psoriasis. The flowers may be eaten raw,
candied or made into a conserve to strengthen people
weakened by prolonged illness.
ADMINISTERED AS: an infusion, poultice or lotion.

Broom *Cytisus scoparius*.
COMMON NAME: broom tops, Irish tops, basam, bizzom,
browne, brum, bream, green broom.
OCCURRENCE: indigenous to England and commonly found
on heathland throughout Britain, Europe and northern Asia.
PARTS USED: the young herbaceous tops, which contain
sparteine and scoparin as the active components.
MEDICINAL USES: diuretic and cathartic. The broom tops may
be used as a decoction or infusion to aid dropsy, while if the
tops are pressed and treated broom juice is obtained. This
fluid extract is generally used in combination with other
diuretic compounds. An infusion of broom, AGRIMONY and
DANDELION root is excellent in remedying bladder, kidney
and liver trouble. *Cytisus* should be used carefully as the
sparteine has a strong effect on the heart and, depending
upon the dose, can cause weakness of the heart similar to
that caused by HEMLOCK (*Conium maculatum*). Death can

occur in extreme cases if the respiratory organ's activity is impaired.

ADMINISTERED AS: fluid extract and infusion.

Burdock *Artium lappa*.

COMMON NAME: lappa, fox's clote, thorny burr, beggar's buttons, cockle buttons, love leaves, philanthropium, personata, happy major, clot-bur.

OCCURRENCE: freely found in ditches and hedgerows throughout England and Europe but rare in Scotland.

PARTS USED: the root, herb and seeds (fruits). They contain the chemicals inulin, mucilage, sugar and tannic acid along with a crystalline glucoside, lappin.

MEDICINAL USES: alterative, diuretic and diaphoretic. It is an excellent blood purifier and very effective in remedying all skin diseases. The root is most powerful and has antiscorbutic properties, which make it very useful for boils, scurvy and rheumatism. Also used as a wash for ulcers and a poultice for tumours, gouty swellings and bruises. An infusion of the leaves aids the stomach and eases indigestion. The tincture obtained from the seeds is a relaxant, demulcent and a tonic for the skin.

ADMINISTERED AS: a fluid extract, infusion, tincture and solid extract.

Butterbur *Petasites vulgaris*.

COMMON NAME: langwort, umbrella plant, bog rhubarb, plapperdock, blatterdock, capdockin, bogshorns, butterdock.

OCCURRENCE: in low wet grounds, marshy meadows and riversides in Great Britain.

PARTS USED: the rhizome, or rootstock.

MEDICINAL USES: as a cardiac tonic, a stimulant, and diuretic. It is good as a remedy for fevers, asthma, colds, urinary complaints, gravel and plague. It is also taken as a homeopathic remedy for severe neuralgia in the back and loins. Recently, the use of butterbur has been recommended in easing the pain of migraine and painful menstruation. One of the most important developments is the treatment of cancer with *Petasites*, where the drug attacks tumours and abnormal cell changes very strongly. In clinical tests, it has been shown to slow or stop the cancer spreading through the body. It has also become an effective remedy for severe asthma.

ADMINISTERED AS: a decoction and tincture.

Cacao *Theobroma cacao.*

COMMON NAME: cocoa, chocolate tree.

OCCURRENCE: found in tropical America and cultivated in most tropical countries, e.g. Sri Lanka and Java

PARTS USED: the seed, which contains about two per cent of the chemical theobromine and forty to sixty per cent solid fat.

MEDICINAL USES: emollient, diuretic, stimulant and nutritive. The seeds are ground into a paste between hot rollers, with sugar and starch being added to produce cocoa. The cocoa butter (or oil of theobroma) produced forms a hard solid that is used in cosmetics, suppositories and coating pills. It has very good emollient qualities and is used to soften chapped hands and lips. The alkaloid theobromine, which is contained in the beans, is similar to caffeine in action on the central nervous system but less powerful. It acts on the heart, kidneys and muscle, and is used as a diuretic and stimulant of the kidneys. This is useful after fluid has accumulated in the body after heart failure, and it is given in conjunction with digitalis (foxglove). The drug is also of benefit in high blood pressure.

ADMINISTERED AS: expressed oil, theobromine.

Camomile *see* Chamomile.

Camphor *Cinnamonum camphora*.

COMMON NAME: gum camphor, laurel camphor, camphire, *Laurus camphora*, *Camphora officinarum*.

OCCURRENCE: found in China, Japan and parts of east Asia.

PARTS USED: the gum and distilled oil.

MEDICINAL USES: sedative, anodyne, antispasmodic, diaphoretic, anthelmintic, aromatic. It is mainly used in colds, chills, fevers, inflammatory complaints and for severe diarrhoea. It is taken internally for hysteria, nervousness, neuralgia and is used as an excitant in cases of heart failure caused by infections, fevers and pneumonia. Camphor is highly valued in all irritations of the sexual organs. Large doses of camphor should be avoided as they can cause vomiting, palpitations and convulsions because of the effects it has on the human brain.

ADMINISTERED AS: tincture, distilled oil, injection, capsules.

Caraway *Carum carvi.*

COMMON NAME: caraway seed, caraway fruit, alcaravea.

OCCURRENCE: common in Europe and Asia and naturalised in Britain.

PARTS USED: the fruit, which produces a volatile oil containing a hydrocarbon, carvene, and an oxygenated oil, carvol.

MEDICINAL USES: aromatic, stimulant and carminative. It was widely used as a cordial to ease dyspepsia and hysteria. The oil is applied to treat flatulence and stomach disorders. Distilled caraway water is used to ease flatulent colic in infants and is an excellent children's medicine. The bruised fruits were used to remove pain from bad earache and also as a poultice to take away bruises. Caraway is widely used as a flavouring for cheeses and seed cakes.

ADMINISTERED AS: a liquid extract and poultice.

Cardamom *Elettaria cardamomum.*

COMMON NAME: Mysore cardamon seeds, malabar cardamom, ebil, kakelah seghar, capalaga, gujalatti elachi, ilachi, ailum, *Amomum cardamomum*, *A. repens*, *Alpina cardamom*, matonia *Cardamomum*, *Cardamomum minus*, *Cardamomi semina*.

OCCURRENCE: native to southern India and cultivated in Sri Lanka.

PARTS USED: the dried ripe seed containing volatile and fixed oil, starch, mucilage, potassium salts, resin and lignin.

MEDICINAL USES: carminative, stimulant, aromatic. They have a warming aromatic effect that is useful in indigestion and flatulence. If chewed, they are said to be good for colic and headaches. Cardamom is used chiefly as a flavouring for cakes, liqueurs, etc, and forms part of curry powder mixtures used in cookery.

ADMINISTERED AS: powdered seeds, tincture and fluid extract.

Castor-oil plant *Ricinus communis*.

COMMON NAME: palma Christi, castor-oil bush.

OCCURRENCE: a native of India but it has been cultivated in many tropical, subtropical and temperate countries around the globe.

PARTS USED: the oil expressed from the seeds.

MEDICINAL USES: cathartic, purgative, laxative, vermifuge, galactogogue. Castor oil is regarded as one of the best laxative and purgative preparations available. It is of particular benefit for children and pregnant women because of its mild action in easing constipation, colic and diarrhoea as a result of slow digestion. The oil expels worms from the body after other suitable remedies have been given. When applied externally, castor oil eases cutaneous complaints such as ringworm, itch and leprosy, while it is used as a carrier oil for solutions of pure alkaloids, e.g. atropine or cocaine, from belladonna (*Atropa belladonna*), so that these

drugs can be used in eye surgery. Castor oil is used for a range of industrial purposes, from soap-making to varnishes.
ADMINISTERED AS: expressed oil.

Catmint *Nepeta cataria*.
COMMON NAME: catnep, nep.
OCCURRENCE: a wild English plant in hedges, field borders and waste ground. It is found on a localised basis in Scotland.
PARTS USED: the herb.
MEDICINAL USES: carminative, tonic, diaphoretic, refrigerant, mildly stimulating and slightly emmenagogue. This herb is good in treating colds, fevers, restlessness and colic. It is also used in nervousness and insanity and to calm children and soothe nightmares when taken as an infusion or conserve. Catmint can be applied to swellings and bruises as a poultice.
ADMINISTERED AS: an infusion, injection or poultice.

Cayenne *Capsicum minimum, Capsicum frutescens*.
COMMON NAME: African pepper, chillies, bird pepper.
OCCURRENCE: native to Zanzibar but is now cultivated in most tropical and subtropical countries, e.g. Sierra Leone, Japan and Madagascar
PARTS USED: the fruit, both fresh and dried.
MEDICINAL USES: stimulant, tonic, carminative, rubefacient. It is possibly the purest and best stimulant in herbal medicine. It produces natural warmth and helps the blood circulation, and eases weakness of the stomach and intestines. Cayenne

is added to tonics and is said to ward off disease and can prevent development of colds and fevers.

ADMINISTERED AS: powdered fruit, tincture, capsules, dietary item.

Celery *Apium graveolens*.

COMMON NAME: smallage, wild celery.

OCCURRENCE: native to southern Europe and cultivated in Britain.

PARTS USED: the ripe seeds, herb and root, of which the seeds contain two oils and apiol.

MEDICINAL USES: carminative, stimulant, diuretic, tonic, nervine and aphrodisiac. It is utilised as a tonic in combination with other herbs, promoting restfulness, sleep and lack of hysteria, and is excellent in relieving rheumatism.

ADMINISTERED AS: fluid extract, essential oil and powdered seeds.

Chamomile *Anthemis nobilis*.

COMMON NAME: Roman chamomile, double chamomile, manzanilla (Spanish), maythen (Saxon).

OCCURRENCE: a low-growing plant found wild in the British Isles.

PARTS USED: the flowers and herb. The active principles therein are a volatile oil, anthemic acid, tannic acid and a glucoside.

MEDICINAL USES: tonic, stomachic, anodyne and antispasmodic. An infusion of chamomile tea is an extremely effective remedy for hysterical and nervous afflictions in women, as well as an emmenagogue. Chamomile has a powerful soothing and sedative effect that is harmless. A tincture is used to cure diarrhoea in children, and it is used with purgatives to prevent griping, and as a tonic it helps dropsy. Externally, it can be applied alone or with other herbs as a poultice to relieve pain, swellings, inflammation and neuralgia. Its strong antiseptic properties make it invaluable for reducing swelling of the face because of abscess or injury. As a lotion, the flowers are good for resolving toothache and earache. The herb itself is an ingredient in herb beers. The use of chamomile can be dated back to ancient Egyptian times when they dedicated the plant to the sun because of its extensive healing properties.

ADMINISTERED AS: decoction, infusion, fluid extract and essential oil.

Chickweed *Stellania media*.

COMMON NAME: starweed, star chickweed, *Alsine media*, passerina.

OCCURRENCE: native to all temperate and northern Arctic regions and is naturalised wherever humans beings have settled. A common weed.

PARTS USED: the whole herb, both fresh and dried.

MEDICINAL USES: demulcent, refrigerant. It is good as a poultice to reduce inflammation and heal indolent ulcers but is most important as an ointment in treating eye problems and cutaneous diseases. It will also benefit scurvy and kidney disorders as an infusion.

ADMINISTERED AS: an infusion, poultice and ointment.

Chicory *Cichonium intybus*.

COMMON NAME: succory, wild succory, hendibeh, barbe de capucin.

OCCURRENCE: common in England and Ireland but rarer in Scotland.

PARTS USED: the root.

MEDICINAL USES: tonic, diuretic and laxative. A decoction of the root has benefit in jaundice, liver problems, gout and rheumatic complaints. The root, when dried, roasted and ground, may be added to coffee or may be drunk on its own as a beverage.

ADMINISTERED AS: a decoction, poultice, syrup or distilled water.

Chives *Allium schoenoprasum*.

COMMON NAME: cives.

OCCURRENCE: native to temperate and northern Europe and Great Britain and has been cultivated over a large area of the northern hemisphere.

PARTS USED: the herb.

MEDICINAL USES: this herb stimulates the appetite and helps digestion during convalescence. It is also said to be effective against infections and to prevent anaemia. They are also widely used in food dishes and add vitamins and colour to many meals.

ADMINISTERED AS: fresh herbs.

Cinnamon *Cinnamomum zeylanicum*.

COMMON NAME: *Lauris cinnamomum*.

OCCURRENCE: native to Sri Lanka but is cultivated in other eastern countries.

PARTS USED: the bark.

MEDICINAL USES: carminative, astringent, stimulant, antiseptic, aromatic. It is used as a local stimulant as a powder and infusion, generally combined with other herbs. Cinnamon stops vomiting and nausea, relieves flatulence and diarrhoea and can also be employed to stop haemorrhage of the womb.

ADMINISTERED AS: powder, distilled water, tincture or an essential oil.

Clover, Red *Trifolium pratense*.

COMMON NAME: trefoil, purple clover.

OCCURRENCE: widely distributed in Britain and Europe.

PARTS USED: the flowers.

MEDICINAL USES: alterative, sedative, antispasmodic. The fluid extract or infusion are excellent in treating bronchial and whooping coughs. External applications of the herb in a poultice have been used on cancerous growths.

ADMINISTERED AS: fluid extract and infusion.

Cloves *Eugenia caryophyllata.*

COMMON NAME: *Eugenia aromatica, Eugenia caryophyllus,* clavos.

OCCURRENCE: grow on the Molucca Islands in the southern Philippines.

PARTS USED: the underdeveloped flowers.

MEDICINAL USES: stimulating, carminative, aromatic. It is given as powder or an infusion for nausea, vomiting, flatulence, languid indigestion and dyspepsia. The volatile oil contains the medicinal properties and it is a strong germicide, antiseptic and a local irritant. It has been used as an expectorant to aid bronchial troubles. Clove oil is often used in association with other medicines.

ADMINISTERED AS: powdered cloves, infusion, essential oil, fluid extract.

Coffee *Coffea arabica.*

COMMON NAME: caffea.

OCCURRENCE: native to a province of Abyssinia and cultivated throughout the tropics.

PARTS USED: the seed and leaves. When roasted, coffee contains oil, wax, caffeine, aromatic oil, tannic acid, caffetannic acid, gum, sugar and protein.

MEDICINAL USES: stimulant, diuretic, anti-narcotic, anti-emetic. Coffee is commonly used as a beverage but it can also be applied as a medicine. It is a brain stimulant, causing sleeplessness, and hence is useful in cases of narcotic poisoning. For this reason it is very good against snake bite in that it helps stop people falling into a coma. Caffeine can be valuable for heart disease and fluid retention, and it is used against drunkenness. As a powerful diuretic, it can help ease gout, rheumatism, gravel and dropsy.

ADMINISTERED AS: beverage, caffeine preparation.

Coriander *Coriandrum sativum.*
OCCURRENCE: indigenous to southern Europe and found occasionally in Britain at riversides, fields and waste ground.
PARTS USED: the fruit and leaves.
MEDICINAL USES: stimulant, aromatic and carminative. It is generally used with active purgatives as flavouring and to lessen their griping tendencies. Coriander water was formerly used for windy colic.
ADMINISTERED AS: powdered fruit, fluid extract.

Cornflower *Centaurea cyanus.*
COMMON NAME: bluebottle, bluebow, hurtsickle, blue cap, bluet.
OCCURRENCE: common in cultivated fields and roadsides in Britain.
PARTS USED: the flowers.
MEDICINAL USES: tonic, stimulant and emmenagogue properties. Water distilled from the petals was said to be a remedy for eye inflammation.
ADMINISTERED AS: distilled water and infusion.

Couchgrass *Agropyrum repens.*

COMMON NAME: twitchgrass, Scotch quelch, quickgrass, dog's grass, *Triticum repens.*

OCCURRENCE: abundant in fields and waste ground in Britain, Europe, northern Asia and North and South America

PARTS USED: the rhizome, which contains triticin (a carbohydrate).

MEDICINAL USES: diuretic, demulcent, aperient. Widely used in complaints of the urinary organs and bladder. Also recommended for gout and rheumatism.

ADMINISTERED AS: an infusion, decoction and liquid extract.

Cowslip *Primula veris.*

COMMON NAME: herb Peter, paigle, peggle, key flower, key of heaven, fairy cups, petty mulleins, patsywort, plumrocks, mayflower, Our Lady's keys, arthritica.

OCCURRENCE: a common wild flower in all parts of Great Britain.

PARTS USED: the flower.

MEDICINAL USES: sedative, antispasmodic. It is very good in relieving restlessness and insomnia. Commonly brewed into a wine, which was a good children's medicine in small doses.

ADMINISTERED AS: an infusion or wine.

Crowfoot, Upright meadow *Ranunculus acris.*

COMMON NAME: gold cup, grenouillette.

OCCURRENCE: native in meadows, pastures and fields in all parts of northern Europe and Great Britain.

PARTS USED: the whole herb.

MEDICINAL USES: the expressed juice is used to remove warts. A poultice of the fresh herb is good at removing violent, painful headaches or in relieving gout. The fresh herb once formed part of a famous cure for cancer practised in 1794.

ADMINISTERED AS: fresh leaves, expressed juice.

Cumin *Cuminum cyminum*.

COMMON NAME: cummin, *Cumino aigro*.

OCCURRENCE indigenous to upper Egypt and cultivated in Arabia, India, China and Mediterranean countries since early times.

PARTS USED: the fruit. The chief constituents are a volatile oil, a fatty oil with resin, mucilage, gum, malates and albuminous matter.

MEDICINAL USES: stimulant, carminative, antispasmodic. This herb has similar effects to fennel and caraway, but its use has declined because of its disagreeable taste. It had a considerable reputation in helping correct flatulence caused by languid digestion and as a remedy for colic and dyspeptic headache. Applied externally as a plaster, it eased stitches and pains in the side and has been combined with other herbs to form a stimulating liniment.

ADMINISTERED AS: dried, powdered fruit, whole fruit.

Daffodil *Narcissus pseudo-narcissus*.

COMMON NAME: narcissus, porillion, daffy-down-dilly, fleur de coucou, Lent lily.

OCCURRENCE: found wild in most European countries including the British Isles.

PARTS USED: the bulb, leaves and flowers. The bulbs contain an alkaloid called lyconine.

MEDICINAL USES: the flowers, when powdered, have emetic properties and as an infusion are used in pulmonary catarrh. The bulbs are also emetic and, indeed, can cause people to collapse and die as a result of paralysis of the central nervous system caused by the action of lyconine, which acts quickly. Accidents have resulted from daffodil bulbs being mistaken for onions and eaten. Since high temperatures and cooking do not break down the poisonous alkaloid, considerable care should be taken to avoid problems. The bulbs are used externally as an astringent poultice to dissolve hard swellings and aid wound healing.

ADMINISTERED AS: powder and extract.

Daisy, Ox-eye *Chrysanthemum leuconthemum*.

COMMON NAME: great ox-eye, goldens, marguerite, moon daisy, horse gowan, maudlin daisy, field daisy, dun daisy, butter daisy, horse daisy, maudlinwort, white weed, gowan.

OCCURRENCE: found in fields throughout Europe and northern Asia.

PARTS USED: the whole herb, flowers and root.

MEDICINAL USES: antispasmodic, diuretic, tonic. This herb's main use has been in whooping cough, asthma and nervous excitability. When taken as a tonic, it acts in a similar way to CHAMOMILE flowers and calms night sweats and nightmares. An infusion of ox-eye daisy flowers is good at relieving bronchial coughs and catarrh. It is also used as a lotion for wounds, bruises and ulcers.

ADMINISTERED AS: an infusion and lotion.

Dandelion *Taraxacum officinale.*
COMMON NAME: priest's crown, swine's snout.
OCCURRENCE: widely found across the northern temperate zone in pastures, meadows and waste ground.
PARTS USED: the root and leaves. The main constituents of the root are taraxacin, a bitter substance, and taraxacerin, an acid resin, along with the sugar inulin.
MEDICINAL USES: diuretic, tonic and slightly aperient. It acts as a general body stimulant but chiefly acts on the liver and kidneys. Dandelion is used as a bitter tonic in atonic dyspepsia, as a mild laxative and to promote increased appetite and digestion. The herb is best used in combination with other herbs and is used in many patent medicines. Roasted dandelion root is also used as a coffee substitute and helps ease dyspepsia, gout and rheumatism.
ADMINISTERED AS: fluid and solid extract, decoction, infusion and tincture.

Dill *Peucedanum graveolus, Fructus anethi.*
COMMON NAME: dill seed, dill fruit, Anethum graveolus, Fructus anethi.

OCCURRENCE: indigenous to Mediterranean districts and southern Russia and is cultivated in England and Europe.

PARTS USED: the dried ripe fruit. An oil obtained from the fruit is almost identical to oil of caraway, both containing limonene and carvone.

MEDICINAL USES: stimulant, aromatic, carminative and stomachic. It is usually given as dill water, which is very good for children's flatulence or disordered digestion.

ADMINISTERED AS: distilled water, essential oil.

Dock, Yellow *Rumex crispus*.
COMMON NAME: curled dock.
OCCURRENCE: normally found on roadside ditches and waste ground all over Great Britain.
PARTS USED: the root and whole herb.
MEDICINAL USES: the root has laxative, alterative and mildly tonic actions and is used in rheumatism, bilious complaints and haemorrhoids. It is very useful in treating jaundice, diseases of the blood, scurvy, chronic skin diseases and as a tonic on the digestive system. Yellow dock is said to have a positive effect on slowing the development of cancer because of its alterative and tonic properties. It has similar effects to that of rhubarb and has been used in treating diphtheria.
ADMINISTERED AS: dried extract, syrup, infusion, tincture, ointment, fluid extract and solid extract.

Dog-rose *Rosa canina*.
COMMON NAME: wild briar, hip tree, cynosbatos.

OCCURRENCE: indigenous to Great Britain.

PARTS USED: the ripe fruit, which contains invert fruit sugars, a range of mineral salts and a large proportion of vitamin C or ascorbic acid.

MEDICINAL USES: astringent, refrigerant and pectoral. The fruit is used in strengthening the stomach and digestion as well as easing coughs. It is made into an uncooked preserve, a syrup that is excellent for infants and children, and rose-hip tea has very beneficial effects. An infusion of dog-rose leaves has been used as a tea substitute and has a pleasant aroma.

ADMINISTERED AS: an infusion, syrup or dietary item.

Elecampane *Inula helenium*.

COMMON NAME: scabwort, elf dock, wild sunflower, horseheal, velvet dock.

OCCURRENCE: a true native of southern England, temperate Europe and Asia, but cultivated in northern Britain.

PARTS USED: the root. This plant is a rich source of the drug inulin.

MEDICINAL USES: diuretic, tonic, diaphoretic, expectorant, antiseptic, astringent, and gently stimulant. It is used principally in coughs, consumption and pulmonary complaints, e.g. bronchitis. It is also used in acute catarrhal afflictions, dyspepsia and asthma. Internally, it is normally combined with other herbs as a decoction. Applied externally, it is a rubefacient and used in treating sciatica and facial neuralgia. The active bitter principle in the herb, helenin, is a very powerful antiseptic and bacterial chemical. This has meant elecampane has been used against the tubercle bacteria and in surgical dressings.

ADMINISTERED AS: powdered root, fluid extract, tincture, poultice, infusion.

Eucalyptus *Eucalyptus globulus.*
COMMON NAME: blue gum tree, stringy bark tree.
OCCURRENCE: native to Australia and Tasmania, now introduced into North and South Africa, India and southern Europe.
PARTS USED: the oil distilled from the leaves. The oil contains eucalyptol, which is the important medically active chemical.
MEDICINAL USES: antiseptic, antispasmodic, stimulant, aromatic. The oil is used as an antiseptic and stimulant gargle; it increases the action of the heart and is said to have some antimalarial properties. It is taken internally in pulmonary tuberculosis, scarlet fever, typhoid and intermittent fevers. The oil is used as an inhalant to clear catarrh and used externally to ease croup and throat troubles. However, in large doses it can irritate the kidneys, depress the nervous system and possibly stop respiration and breathing. Despite its harmless appearance, care should be used when administering the drug internally.

ADMINISTERED AS: distilled oil, emulsion.

Evening primrose *Oenothera biennis.*
COMMON NAME: tree primrose, sun drop.

OCCURRENCE: native to North America but has been naturalised to British and European gardens.

PARTS USED: the bark and leaves.

MEDICINAL USES: astringent, sedative. The drug from this herb is not extensively used but has been of benefit in treating gastro-intestinal disorders, dyspepsia, liver torpor and in female problems in association with pelvic illness. It has also been successfully used in whooping cough and spasmodic asthma.

ADMINISTERED AS: liquid extract.

Fennel *Foeniculum vulgare*.

COMMON NAME: hinojo, fenkel, sweet fennel, wild fennel.

OCCURRENCE: found wild in most areas of temperate Europe and generally considered indigenous to the shores of the Mediterranean. It is cultivated for medicinal benefit in France, Russia, India and Persia.

PARTS USED: the seeds, leaves and roots. The roots are rarely used today. The essential oil is separated by distillation with water. Fennel oil varies widely in quality and composition, dependent on where and under what conditions the fennel was grown.

MEDICINAL USES: aromatic, stimulant, carminative and stomachic. The herb is principally used with purgatives to allay their tendency to griping, and the seeds form an ingredient of the compound liquorice powder. Fennel water also acts in a similar manner to DILL water in correcting infant flatulence.

ADMINISTERED AS: fluid extract, distilled water, essential oil.

Fenugreek *Trigonella foenum-graecum*.

COMMON NAME: bird's foot, Greek hay-seed.

OCCURRENCE: indigenous to eastern Mediterranean countries but is cultivated in India, Africa and England.

PARTS USED: the seeds. These contain mucilage, two alkaloids – trigonelline and choline – phosphates, lecithin and nucleoalbumin.

MEDICINAL USES: a preparation where seeds are soaked in water until they swell and form a thick paste is used to prevent fevers, is comforting to the stomach and has been utilised for diabetes. Alcoholic tinctures are used to prepare emollient cream, ointments and plasters, while the mucilage is used externally as a poultice for skin infections such as abscesses, boils and carbuncles. It is also good at relieving rickets, anaemia and scrofula, while, combined with the normal dosage of conventional medicine, e.g insulin, it is helpful in gout, diabetes and neurasthenia. It is widely used as a flavouring for both human and cattle feed.

ADMINISTERED AS: poultice, ointment, infusion or tincture.

Feverfew *Chrysanthemum parthenium*.

COMMON NAME: featherfew, featherfoil, flirtwort, bachelor's buttons, *Pyrethrum parthenium*.

OCCURRENCE: a wild hedgerow plant found in many areas of Europe and Great Britain.

PARTS USED: the herb.

MEDICINAL USES: aperient, carminative, bitter, stimulant,

emmenagogue. It is employed for hysterical complaints, nervousness and low spirits as a general tonic. A decoction is made and is useful in easing coughs, wheezing and difficult breathing. Earache was relieved by a cold infusion, while a tincture of feverfew eased the pain and swelling caused after insect or vermin bites. The herb was planted around dwellings to purify the atmosphere and ward off disease. Today, it is used to prevent or ease migraines or headaches.

ADMINISTERED AS: warm or cold infusion, poultice, tincture, decoction.

Foxglove *Digitalis purpurea.*
COMMON NAME: witch's gloves, dead men's bells, fairy's glove, gloves of Our Lady, bloody fingers, virgin's glove, fairy caps, folk's glove, fairy thimbles, fair women's plant.
OCCURRENCE: indigenous and widely distributed throughout Great Britain and Europe.
PARTS USED: the leaves, which contain four important glucosides – digitoxin, digitalin, digitalein and digitonin – of which the first three listed are cardiac stimulants.
MEDICINAL USES: cardiac tonic, sedative, diuretic. Administering digitalis increases the activity of all forms of muscle tissue, particularly the heart and arterioles. It causes a very high rise in blood pressure and the pulse is slowed and becomes regular. Digitalis causes the heart to contract in size, allowing increased blood flow and nutrient delivery

to the organ. It also acts on the kidneys and is a good remedy for dropsy, particularly when it is connected with cardiac problems. The drug has benefits in treating internal haemorrhage, epilepsy, inflammatory diseases and delirium tremens. Digitalis has a cumulative action whereby it is liable to accumulate in the body and then have poisonous effects. It should only be used under medical advice. Digitalis is an excellent antidote in aconite poisoning when given as a hypodermic injection.

ADMINISTERED AS: tincture, infusion, powdered leaves, solid extract, injection.

Garlic *Allium sativum*.
COMMON NAME: poor man's treacle.
OCCURRENCE: cultivated throughout Europe since antiquity.
PARTS USED: the bulb.
MEDICINAL USES: antiseptic, diaphoretic, diuretic, expectorant, stimulant. It may be externally applied as ointment, lotion, antiseptic or as a poultice. Syrup of garlic is very good for asthma, coughs, difficulty in breathing and chronic bronchitis, while fresh juice has been used to ease tubercular consumption. The essential oil is commonly taken as a supplement in the form of gelatine capsules. Several species of wild garlic are utilised for both medicinal and dietary purposes.

ADMINISTERED AS: expressed juice, syrup, tincture, essential oil, poultice, lotion and ointment.

Ginger *Zingiber officinale*.

OCCURRENCE: a native of Asia, it is now cultivated in the West Indies, Jamaica and Africa.

PARTS USED: the root, which contains volatile oil, two resins, gum, starch, lignin, acetic acid and asmazone as well as several unidentified compounds.

MEDICINAL USES: stimulant, carminative, expectorant. A valuable herb in dyspepsia, flatulent colic, alcoholic gastritis and diarrhoea. Ginger tea is taken to relieve the effects of cold temperatures, including triggering normal menstruation patterns in women. Ginger is also used to flavour bitter infusions, cough mixtures or syrups.

ADMINISTERED AS: infusion, fluid extract, tincture and syrup.

Ginseng *Panax quinquefolium*.

COMMON NAME: *Aralia quinquefolia*, five fingers, tartar root, red berry, man's health, panax, pannag.

OCCURRENCE: native to certain areas of China, eastern Asia and North America. It is largely cultivated in China, Korea and Japan.

PARTS USED: the root, which contains a large quantity of gum, resin, volatile oil and the peculiar sweetish compound panaquilon.

MEDICINAL USES: mild stomachic, tonic, stimulant. The generic name, *Panax*, is derived from the Greek for panacea, meaning 'all-healing'. The name ginseng is said to mean 'the wonder of the world', and the Chinese consider this herb a sovereign remedy in all diseases. It is good in dyspepsia, vomiting and nervous disorders, consumption and exhaustion. In the West, it is used to treat loss of appetite and stomach and digestive problems, possibly arising from nervous and mental exhaustion. Ginseng is considered to work well against fatigue, old age and its infirmities and to help convalescents recover their health. In healthy people, the drug is said to increase vitality, cure pulmonary complaints and tumours and increase life expectancy. It was also used by the native American Indians for similar problems.

ADMINISTERED AS: tincture, decoction, capsules.

Golden rod *Solidago virgaurea.*

COMMON NAME: verge d'or, solidago, goldruthe, woundwort, Aaron's rod.

OCCURRENCE: normally found wild in woods in Britain, Europe, central Asia and North America but it is also a common garden plant.

PARTS USED: the leaves contain tannin, with some bitter and astringent chemicals that are unknown.

MEDICINAL USES: aromatic, stimulant, carminative. This herb is astringent and diuretic and is highly effective in curing gravel and urinary stones. It aids weak digestion, stops sickness and is very good against diphtheria. As a warm infusion it is a good diaphoretic drug and is used as such to help painful menstruation and amenorrhoea (absence or stopping of menstrual periods).

ADMINISTERED AS: fluid extract, infusion, spray.

Guarana *Paullinia cupara*.

COMMON NAME: Paullina, guarana bread, Brazilian cocoa, uabano, uaranzeiro, *Paullina sorbilis*.

OCCURRENCE: native to Brazil and Uruguay.

PARTS USED: the prepared seed, crushed. The seeds are shelled, roasted for six hours and shaken until their outer shell comes off. They are ground to a fine powder, made into a dough with water and formed into cylinders that are dried in the sun or over a fire. The seed preparation is eaten with water by the native people. The roasted seeds contain caffeine, tannic acid, catechutannic acid, starch and a fixed oil.

MEDICINAL USES: nervine, tonic, stimulant, aphrodisiac, febrifuge, slightly narcotic. It is used in mild forms of diarrhoea or leucorrhoea and also for headaches, in particular those linked to the menstrual cycle. Guarana stimulates the brain after mental exertion, or after fatigue or exhaustion caused by hot temperatures. It may also have diuretic effects where it can help rheumatism, lumbago and bowel complaints. The drug is similar to that of coca or coffee.

ADMINISTERED AS: powder, fluid extract, tincture.

Hemlock *Conium maculatum*.

COMMON NAME: herb bennet, spotted conebane, musquash root, beaver poison, poison hemlock, poison parsley, spotted hemlock, vex, vecksies.

OCCURRENCE: common in hedges, meadows, waste ground

and stream banks throughout Europe and is also found in temperate Asia and North Africa.

PARTS USED: the leaves, fruits and seeds. The most important constituent of hemlock leaves is the alkaloid coniine, which is poisonous with a disagreeable odour. Other alkaloids in the plant include methyl-coniine, conhydrine, pseudoconhydrine, ethyl piperidine.

MEDICINAL USES: sedative, antispasmodic, anodyne. The drug acts on the centres of motion and causes paralysis, so it is used to remedy undue nervous motor excitability, e.g. teething, cramp and muscle spasms of the larynx and gullet. When inhaled, hemlock is said to be good in relieving coughs, bronchitis, whooping cough and asthma. The method of action of *Conium* means it is directly antagonistic to the effects of strychnine, from nux vomica (*Strychnos nux-vomica*), and hence it is used as an antidote to strychnine poisoning and similar poisons. Hemlock has to be administered with care as narcotic poisoning may result from internal application and overdoses induce paralysis, with loss of speech and depression of respiratory function leading to death. Antidotes to hemlock poisoning are tannic acid, stimulants, e.g. coffee, mustard and castor oil.

ADMINISTERED AS: powdered leaves, fluid extract, tincture, expressed juice of the leaves and solid extract.

Hops *Humulus lupulus*.

OCCURRENCE: a native British plant, found wild in hedges

and woods from Yorkshire southward. It is considered an introduced species to Scotland but is also found in most countries of the northern temperate zone.

PARTS USED: the flowers, which contain a volatile oil, two bitter principles – lupamaric acid, lupalinic acid – and tannin.

MEDICINAL USES: tonic, nervine, diuretic, anodyne, aromatic. The volatile oil has sedative and soporific effects while the bitter principles are stomachic and tonic. Hops are used to promote the appetite and enhance sleep. An infusion is very effective in heart disease, fits, neuralgia, indigestion, jaundice, nervous disorders and stomach or liver problems. Hop juice is a blood cleanser and is very effective in remedying calculus problems. As an external application, hops are used with CHAMOMILE heads as an infusion to reduce painful swellings or inflammation and bruises. This combination may also be used as a poultice.

ADMINISTERED AS: an infusion, tincture, poultice, expressed juice or tea.

Horseradish *Cochlearia armoracia*.

COMMON NAME: mountain radish, great raifort, red cole, *Armoracia rusticara*.

OCCURRENCE: cultivated in the British Isles for centuries. The place of origin is unknown.

PARTS USED: the root, which contains the glucoside sinigrin, vitamin C, aspargin and resin.

MEDICINAL USES: stimulant, aperient, rubefacient, diuretic, antiseptic, diaphoretic. Horseradish is a powerful stimulant of the digestive organs, and it acts on lung and urinary infections, clearing them away. The herb is a very strong diuretic and, as such, is used to ease dropsy, gravel and calculus as well as being taken internally for gout and rheumatism. A poultice can be made from the fresh root and applied to rheumatic joints and chilblains, and to ease facial neuralgia. Horseradish juice, when diluted with vinegar and glycer ine, was used in children's whooping cough and to relieve hoarseness of the throat. An infusion of the root in urine was stimulating to the entire nervous system and promoted perspiration, while it was also used to expel worms in children. Care should be taken when using this herb because over-use of horseradish can blister the skin, and it is not suitable for people with thyroid troubles.

ADMINISTERED AS: infusion, syrup, expressed juice, fluid extract.

Ipecacuanha *Cephaelis ipecacuanha.*
COMMON NAME: *Psychotria ipecacuanha.*
OCCURRENCE: a native of Brazil, Bolivia and other parts of South America, ipecacuanha was first introduced into Europe in the 17th century.
PARTS USED: the chief constituents of the root are the alkaloids emetrine, cephaelin and psychotrine, as well as two glucosides, choline, resin, calcium oxalate and a volatile oil, among other compounds.

MEDICINAL USES: diaphoretic, emetic, expectorant, stimulant. The effects of the drug on the body are entirely dependent on the dose given. In very small doses, ipecacuanha stimulates the stomach, liver and intestine, aiding digestion and increasing appetite, while in slightly larger doses it has diaphoretic and expectorant properties that are good for colds, coughs and dysentery. Large doses of the drug are emetic. There is a lot of historical use of this drug against amoebic (or tropical) dysentery, where rapid cures can occur. Care should be taken in utilising this drug as emetine can have a toxic effect on the heart, blood vessels, lungs and intestines and can cause severe illness.

ADMINISTERED AS: powdered root, fluid extract, tincture, syrup.

Ivy *Hedera helix*.

COMMON NAME: common ivy.

OCCURRENCE: native to many parts of Europe and northern and central Asia.

PARTS USED: the leaves and berries.

MEDICINAL USES: stimulating, diaphoretic, cathartic. The leaves have been used as poultices on enlarged glands, ulcers and abscesses and the berries ease fevers and were used extensively during the Great Plague of London.

ADMINISTERED AS: poultice, infusion.

Ivy, Poison *Rhus toxicodendron*.

COMMON NAME: poison oak, poison vine.

OCCURRENCE: native to the United States of America.

PARTS USED: the fresh leaves, which contain a resin called toxicodendron as the active principle.

MEDICINAL USES: irritant, rubefacient, stimulant, narcotic. This herb is successful in treating obstinate skin eruptions, palsy, paralysis, acute rheumatism and joint stiffness. It has also been good in treating ringworm, allergic rashes and urinary incontinence. In small doses, poison ivy is a very good sedative for the nervous system, but care must be taken in its use as it can trigger gastric and intestinal irritation, drowsiness, stupor and delirium.

ADMINISTERED AS: tincture, fluid extract, infusion.

Juniper *Juniperus communis.*

OCCURRENCE: a common shrub native to Great Britain and widely distributed through many parts of the world.

PARTS USED: the berry and leaves.

MEDICINAL USES: the oil of juniper obtained from the ripe berries is stomachic, diuretic and carminative and is used to treat indigestion and flatulence as well as kidney and bladder diseases. The main use of juniper is in dropsy and aiding other diuretic herbs to ease the disease.

ADMINISTERED AS: essential oil from berries, essential oil from wood, fluid extract, liquid extract, solid extract.

Kamala *Mallotus philippinensis.*

COMMON NAME: *Glandulae rottelerde*, kamcela, spoonwood, *Röttlera tinctoria*, kameela.

OCCURRENCE: native to India, Abyssinia, southern Arabia, China and Australia.

PARTS USED: the powder removed from the capsular fruit, composed of hairs and glands.

MEDICINAL USES: taeniafuge, purgative. The powder kills and expels tapeworms from the body. The worm is usually removed whole. It is a quick and active purgative drug, causing griping and nausea. It is used externally for cutaneous complaints, including scabies and herpetic ringworm.

ADMINISTERED AS: powdered kamala, fluid extract.

Kola nuts *Kola vera*.

COMMON NAME: guru nut, cola, kola seeds, gurru nuts, bissy nuts, cola seeds, Cola acuminata, Sterculia acuminata.

OCCURRENCE: native to Sierra Leone and northern Ashanti in Ghana and cultivated in tropical western Africa, West Indies, Brazil and Java.

PARTS USED: the seeds.

MEDICINAL USES: nerve stimulant, diuretic, cardiac tonic. This drug is a good overall tonic, largely because of the caffeine it contains. It has been used as a remedy for diarrhoea and for those with an alcoholic habit.

ADMINISTERED AS: powdered seeds, tincture, fluid and solid extract.

Laburnum *Cytisus laburnam*.

COMMON NAME: yellow laburnum.

OCCURRENCE: indigenous to high mountain regions of Europe and widely cultivated across the globe as a garden plant.

PARTS USED: the alkaloid, obtained from the plant, called cytisine.

MEDICINAL USES: all parts of the laburnum are thought to be poisonous, particularly the seeds. The alkaloid has been recommended in whooping cough and asthma, and also as an insecticide, but it has not been used because of the very poisonous nature of the compound. Laburnum poisoning symptoms include intense sleepiness, vomiting, convulsive movements, coma and unequally dilated pupils. Laburnum is also poisonous to cattle and horses, and deaths of both livestock and humans have resulted from ingestion of this plant.

Lavender, English *Lavandula vera.*

OCCURRENCE: indigenous to mountainous regions in the western Mediterranean and is cultivated extensively in France, Italy, England and Norway.

PARTS USED: the flowers and the essential oil, which contains linalool, linalyl acetate, cineol, pinene, limonene and tannin

MEDICINAL USES: aromatic, carminative, stimulant, nervine. It is mainly used as a flavouring agent for disagreeable odours in ointments or syrups. The essential oil when taken internally is restorative and a tonic against faintness, heart palpitations, giddiness and colic. It raises the spirits, promotes the appetite and dispels flatulence. When applied externally, the oil relieves toothache, neuralgia, sprains and rheumatism. The oil is utilised widely in aromatherapy, often to very beneficial effect.

ADMINISTERED AS: fluid extract, tincture, essential oil, spirit, infusion, tea, poultice, distilled water.

Lemon *Citrus limonica*.

COMMON NAME: limon, *Citrus medica*, *Citrus limonum*, citronnier, neemoo, leemoo, limoun, limone.

OCCURRENCE: indigenous to northern India and widely cultivated in Mediterranean countries.

PARTS USED: the fruit, rind, juice and oil. Lemon peel contains an essential oil and a bitter principle, while lemon juice is rich in citric acid, sugar and gum. Oil of lemon contains the aldehyde citral and the oils pinene and citronella.

MEDICINAL USES: antiscorbutic, tonic, refrigerant, cooling. Lemon juice is the best preventative drug for scurvy and is also very valuable in fevers and allaying thirst. It is recommended in acute rheumatism and may be given to counteract narcotic poisons such as opium. It is used as an astringent gargle in sore throats, for uterine haemorrhage after childbirth, as a lotion in sunburn and as a cure for severe hiccups. The juice is also good for jaundice and heart palpitations. A decoction of lemon is a good antiperiodic drug and can be used to replace quinine in malarial injections or to reduce the temperature in typhoid fever. Lemon oil is a strong external rubefacient and also has stomachic and carminative qualities.

ADMINISTERED AS: syrup, decoction, fresh juice, tincture, essential oil, dietary item.

Lily of the valley *Convallaria magalis.*

COMMON NAME: May lily, convarraria, Our Lady's tears, conval lily, lily constancy, ladder to heaven, Jacob's ladder.

OCCURRENCE: native to Europe and distributed over North America and northern Asia. It is very localised in England and Scotland.

PARTS USED: the flowers, leaves and whole herb. The chief constituents are two glucosides – convallamarin (the active principle) and convallarin – as well as tannin and mineral salts.

MEDICINAL USES: cardiac tonic, diuretic. A similar drug to digitalis, from the foxglove, although it is less powerful. Strongly recommended in valvular heart disease, cardiac debility and dropsy, and it slows the action of a weak, irritated heart. Lily of the valley does not have accumulatory effects and can be taken in full and frequent doses without harm. A decoction of the flowers is good at removing obstructions in the urinary canal.

ADMINISTERED AS: fluid extracts, decoction tincture, powdered flowers.

Lily, Madonna *Lilium candidum.*
COMMON NAME: white lily, meadow lily.
OCCURRENCE: a southern European native that has been cultivated in Great Britain and America for centuries.
PARTS USED: the bulb.
MEDICINAL USES: demulcent, astringent, mucilaginous. The bulb is mainly used as an emollient poultice for ulcers, tumours and external inflammation. When made into an ointment, Madonna lily removes corns and eliminates pain and inflammation from burns and scalds, reducing scarring. When used in combination with life root (Senecio aureus), Madonnna lily is of great value in treating leucorrhoea, prolapse of the womb and other female complaints. The bulb is very often eaten as a food in Japan.
ADMINISTERED AS: poultice, ointment, decoction.

Lime fruit *Citrus medica* var. *acida.*
COMMON NAME: Citrus acris, Citrus acida, limettae fructus.
OCCURRENCE: a native Asian tree that is cultivated in many warm countries, including in the West Indies and Italy.
PARTS USED: the fruit and juice.
MEDICINAL USES: refrigerant, antiscorbutic. The juice of the lime contains citric acid and is a popular beverage, sweetened as a syrup. It is used to treat dyspepsia.
ADMINISTERED AS: fresh juice, syrup

Lime tree *Tilia europoea.*
COMMON NAME: linden flowers, linn flowers, common lime,

tilleul, flores tiliae, *Tilia vulgaris, T. intermedia, T. cordata, T. platyphylla.*

OCCURRENCE: native to the British Isles and the northern temperate zone.

PARTS USED: the lime flowers, bark, powdered charcoal. The flowers contain volatile oil, flavonid glucosides, saponins, condensed tannins and mucilage.

MEDICINAL USES: nervine, stimulant, tonic. An infusion of the flowers is good for indigestion, hysteria, nervous vomiting, colds, 'flu and catarrh. They can also help calm overactive children and relax the nervous system. Lime-flower tea eases headaches and insomnia. The flowers are said to lower blood pressure (possibly because of the bioflavonoids they contain) and are said to remedy arteriosclerosis. The inner bark of the lime has a diuretic effect and is utilised for gout and kidney stones as well as treating coronary artery disease by dilating the coronary arteries. The powdered charcoal was used in gastric and dyspeptic disorders and applied to burnt or sore areas.

ADMINISTERED AS: infusion, powdered charcoal, dried inner bark, tea.

Liquorice *Glycyrrhiza glabra.*

COMMON NAME: licorice, lycorys, *Liquiriha officinalis.*

OCCURRENCE: a shrub native to southeast Europe and southwestAsia and cultivated in the British Isles

PARTS USED: the root. The chief compound in the root is

glycyrrhizin along with sugar, starch, gum, asparagus, tannin and resin.

MEDICINAL USES: demulcent, pectoral, emollient. A very popular and well-known remedy for coughs, consumption and chest complaints. Liquorice extract is included in cough lozenges and pastilles, with sedatives and expectorants. An infusion of bruised root and flax (linseed) is good for irritable coughs, sore throats and laryngitis. Liquorice is used to a greater extent as a medicine in China and other eastern countries. The herb is used by brewers to give colour to beer and stout and is employed in the manufacture of chewing or smoking tobacco.

ADMINISTERED AS: powdered root, fluid extract, infusion, solid extract.

Male fern *Dryopteris felix-mas.*

COMMON NAME: *Aspidium felix-mas*, male shield fern.

OCCURRENCE: grows in all areas of Europe, temperate Asia, northern India, North and South Africa, the temperate areas of the United States and the South American Andes.

PARTS USED: the root and the oil extracted from it. The oil is extracted using ether and contains the acid filmaron, filicic acid, tannin, resin and sugar.

MEDICINAL USES: anthelmintic, vermifuge, taeniafuge. It is probably the best drug against tapeworm. It is normally given at night after several hours of fasting. When followed by a purgative drug in the morning, e.g. castor oil, very good results are obtained. The size of the dose administered must be carefully assessed as male fern is an irritant poison in too large a dose, causing muscle weakness, coma and possible damage to the eyesight.

ADMINISTERED AS: powdered root, fluid extract; oil of male fern.

Marigold *Calendula officinalis.*

COMMON NAME: *Caltha officinalis*, golds, ruddes, marg gowles, oculus Christi, marygold, garden marigold, solis sponsa.

OCCURRENCE: a native of southern Europe and a common garden plant in Great Britain.

PARTS USED: the petals and herb. Only the deep orange-flowered variety is of medicinal use.

MEDICINAL USES: stimulant, diaphoretic. Mainly used as a local remedy. Taken internally, an infusion of the herb prevents pus formation and externally is good in cleaning chronic ulcers and varicose veins. Formerly considered to be of benefit as an aperient and detergent to clear visceral obstructions and jaundice. A marigold flower, when rubbed onto a bee or wasp sting, was known to relieve pain and reduce swelling, while a lotion from the flowers was good for inflamed and sore eyes. The expressed juice of the plant was used to clear headaches and remove warts.

ADMINISTERED AS: infusion, distilled water and lotion.

Marjoram *Origanum vulgare.*

OCCURRENCE: generally distributed over Asia, Europe and North Africa and also found freely in England.

PARTS USED: the herb and volatile oil.

MEDICINAL USES: the oil has stimulant, carminative, diaphoretic, mildly tonic and emmenagogue qualities. As a warm infusion, it is used to produce perspiration and bring out the spots of measles as well as giving relief from spasms, colic and dyspeptic pain. The oil has been used externally as a rubefacient and liniment, and on cotton wool placed next to an aching tooth it relieves the pain. The dried herb may be utilised as a hot poultice for swellings, rheumatism and colic, while an infusion of the fresh plant will ease a nervous headache.

ADMINISTERED AS: essential oil, poultice and infusion.

Marshmallow *Althaea officinalis.*

COMMON NAME: mallards, mauls, schloss tea, cheeses, mortification root, guimauve.

OCCURRENCE: a native of Europe, found in salt marshes, meadows, ditches and riverbanks. It is locally distributed in England and has been introduced into Scotland.

PARTS USED: the leaves, root and flowers. It contains starch, mucilage, pectin, oil, sugar, asparagin, glutinous matter and cellulose.

MEDICINAL USES: demulcent, emollient. Very useful in inflammation and irritation of the alimentary canal and the urinary and respiratory organs. A decoction of the root is effective against sprains, bruises or any muscle aches. When boiled in milk or wine, marshmallow relieves diseases of the chest, e.g. coughs, bronchitis or whooping cough, and it eases the bowels after dysentery without any astringent effects. It is frequently given as a syrup to infants and children.

ADMINISTERED AS: infusion, decoction, syrup, fluid extract.

Meadowsweet *Spiraea ulmaria*.

COMMON NAME: meadsweet, dolloff, queen of the meadow, bridewort, lady of the meadow.

OCCURRENCE: common in the British Isles in meadows or woods.

PARTS USED: the herb.

MEDICINAL USES: aromatic, astringent, diuretic, alterative. This herb is good against diarrhoea, stomach complaints and blood disorders. It is highly recommended for children's diarrhoea and dropsy and was used as a decoction in wine to reduce fevers. Meadowsweet makes a pleasant everyday drink when infused and sweetened with honey. It is also included in many herb beers.

ADMINISTERED AS: infusion, decoction.

Mescal buttons *Anhalonicum lewinii*.

COMMON NAME: *Lopophora lewinii*, *Analonium williamsii*, *Echinacactus lewinii*, *Echinocactus williamsii*, pellote, muscal buttons.

OCCURRENCE: Mexico and Texas, USA.

PARTS USED: the tops of the cactus plant. The drug contains four alkaloids – anhalonine, mescaline, anhalonidine and lophophorine – as well as the chemicals pellotine and anhalamine.

MEDICINAL USES: cardiac, tonic, narcotic, emetic. The drug is useful in head injuries, hysteria, asthma, gout, neuralgia and rheumatism. The extracted compound pellotine has been used to induce sleep in people with insanity as it has no undesirable reactions. Large doses of mescal buttons produce an odd cerebral excitement with visual disturbances. The physical effects include muscular relaxation, wakefulness, nausea, vomiting and dilation of the pupil. The ancient Aztec Indians believed mescal buttons to have divine properties and included its use to produce exaltation in their religious ceremonies.

ADMINISTERED AS: fluid extract, tincture, extracted alkaloid.

Mistletoe *Viscum album.*
COMMON NAME: European mistletoe, bird lime mistletoe, herbe de la croix, mystyldene, lignum crucis.
OCCURRENCE: an evergreen, true parasitic plant found on several tree species, including fruit and oak trees. It is found throughout Europe and Britain except in Scotland, where it is very rare.
PARTS USED: the leaves and young twigs. They contain mucilage, sugar, fixed oil, tannin and viscin, the active part of the plant.

MEDICINAL USES: nervine, antispasmodic, tonic and narcotic. It is highly recommended for epilepsy and other convulsive disorders, along with stopping internal haemorrhage. It has also been used in delirium, hysteria, neuralgia, nervous debility, urinary disorders and many other complaints arising from a weakened state of the nervous system. The berries are taken to cure severe stitches in the side, and the plant produces a sticky substance, called bird lime, that is applied to ulcers and sores. Mistletoe is excellent for reducing blood pressure and has been indicated to be a successful cure for chronic arthritis and in treating malignant tumours in the body.

ADMINISTERED AS: tincture, powdered leaves, infusion, fluid extract.

Myrrh *Commiphora molmol.*
COMMON NAME: *Balsamodendron myrrha*, *Commiphora myrrha* var. *molmol*, mira, morr.
OCCURRENCE: obtained from bushes in northeast Africa and in Arabia.
PARTS USED: the oleo-gum resin, which contains volatile oil, resins and gum.
MEDICINAL USES: stimulant, tonic, healing, antiseptic, astringent, expectorant, emmenagogue. Myrrh has a long history of use in countering poisons and putrid tissues throughout the body. It is used in leucorrhoea, chronic catarrh, thrush, athlete's foot, absence of menstrual periods,

ulcers and as a vermifuge. The resin acts as a tonic in dyspepsia, stimulates the circulation, appetite and the production of gastric juices. It makes a very good gargle or mouthwash for an inflamed sore throat, spongy gums and mouth ulcers.

ADMINISTERED AS: fluid extract, tincture, pills.

Nettle *Urtica dioica, Urtica urens.*
COMMON NAME: common nettle, stinging nettle.
OCCURRENCE: widely distributed throughout temperate Europe and Asia, Japan, South Africa and Australia.
PARTS USED: the whole herb, which contains formic acid, mucilage, mineral salts, ammonia and carbonic acid.
MEDICINAL USES: astringent, stimulating, diuretic, tonic. The herb is anti-asthmatic, and the juice of the nettle will relieve bronchial and asthmatic troubles, as will the dried leaves when burnt and inhaled. The seeds are taken as an infusion or in wine to ease consumption or ague. Nettles are used widely as a food source. A hair tonic or lotion can also be made from the nettle. In the Highlands of Scotland, they were chopped, added to egg white and applied to the temples as a cure for insomnia.

ADMINISTERED AS: expressed juice, infusion, decoction, seeds, dried herb, dietary item.

Nightshade, Black *Solarum nignum.*
COMMON NAME: garden nightshade, petty morel.

OCCURRENCE: a common plant in south England, seen less frequently in northern England and Scotland.

PARTS USED: the whole plant, fresh leaves. Both contain the active principle solanine, which is found in variable quantities within the plant throughout the year.

MEDICINAL USES: the bruised fresh leaves are used externally to the body to ease pain and reduce inflammation. Juice of the leaves has been used for ringworm, gout and earache, and is supposed to make a good gargle or mouthwash when mixed with vinegar. This species of plant is reputed to be very poisonous, narcotic and sudorific, so is utilised only in very small doses under careful supervision.

ADMINISTERED AS: infusion, expressed juice and fresh leaves.

Nux vomica *Strychnos nux-vomica.*

COMMON NAME: poison nut, semen strychnox, Quaker buttons.

OCCURRENCE: a tree indigenous to India and now cultivated medicinally in Burma, China, Australia and the Malay Archipelago.

PARTS USED: the dried ripe seeds. They contain the alkaloids strychnine, brucine and strychnicine, fatty matter, caffeotannic acid and the glucoside loganin.

MEDICINAL USES: tonic, bitter, stimulant. Nux vomica is utilised as a general tonic, mainly when combined with other herbal remedies, to treat neuralgia, dyspepsia, impotence, constipation and general debility. This drug can also be of benefit in cardiac failure, surgical shock or poisoning by chloroform, where it raises blood pressure and increases pulse rate, but it can also cause violent convulsions. Nux vomica should only be used under strict control as strychnine is very poisonous.

ADMINISTERED AS: fluid extract, tincture.

Oats *Avena sativa.*

COMMON NAME: groats, oatmeal.

OCCURRENCE: distributed across Europe, Britain and the USA.

PARTS USED: the seeds, which are made up of starch, gluten, albumen and other proteins, sugar, gum oil and salts.

MEDICINAL USES: nervine, stimulant, antispasmodic, *Avena* forms a nutritious and easily digested food for convalescent patients. It can be made into a demulcent enema or an emollient poultice. Oat extract or tincture is useful as a nerve and uterine tonic.

ADMINISTERED AS: fluid extract, tincture, enema, dietary item.

Olive *Olea europea.*

COMMON NAME: *Olea oleaster, O. larcifolia, O. gallica*, oliver.

OCCURRENCE: native to the Mediterranean countries, Syria and Turkey. Now cultivated in Chile, Peru and Australia.

PARTS USED: the oil expressed from the ripe fruit, the leaves.

MEDICINAL USES: the oil is emollient, demulcent, laxative and aperient. It is a good substitute for castor oil when given to children, but its value in clearing parasitic worms or gallstones is unsure. The oil is a good ingredient in liniments or ointment and is used for bruises, sprains, cutaneous injuries and rheumatic problems. It is also utilised externally in joint, kidney and chest complaints or for chills, typhoid and scarlet fevers, plague and dropsy. When combined with alcohol, the oil is good as a hair tonic. Olive leaves have astringent and antiseptic properties, and an infusion of these leaves has proved beneficial in obstinate fevers.

ADMINISTERED AS: expressed oil, infusion, ointment.

Orris *Iris florentina* (and other species).
COMMON NAME: Florentine orris, orris root.
OCCURRENCE: grown in Italy and Morocco and to a smaller extent in England.
PARTS USED: the root contains oil of orris, fat, resin, starch, mucilage, a glucoside called iridin and a bitter extractive substance.
MEDICINAL USES: Orris root is rarely used in medicine today. The fresh root has emetic, diuretic and cathartic properties and was formerly used against congested headache, dropsy, bronchitis and chronic diarrhoea. It is more generally used in perfumery, as it strengthens the odour of other fragrant herbs and acts as a fixative in both perfumes and pot pourri. It is also part of dusting powders, toilet powders and tooth powders.

Parsley *Carum petroselinum*.
COMMON NAME: *Apium petroselinum*, *Petroselinum lativum*, petersylinge, persely, persele.
OCCURRENCE: this was first cultivated in Britain in 1548 and

is now completely naturalised through England and Scotland.

PARTS USED: the root, seeds and leaves. The root is slightly aromatic and contains starch, mucilage, sugar, volatile oil and apiin. Parsley seeds contain more volatile oil, which consists of terpenes and apiol, an allyl compound.

MEDICINAL USES: carminative, tonic, aperient, diuretic. A strong decoction of the root is used in gravel, stone, kidney congestion, jaundice and dropsy. Bruised parsley seeds used to be given against plague and intermittent fevers, while the external application of the leaves may help to dispel tumours. A poultice of the leaves is effective against bites and stings of poisonous insects.

ADMINISTERED AS: fluid extract, essential oil, infusion, ointment and poultice.

Pepper *Piper nigrum.*
COMMON NAME: black pepper, piper.
OCCURRENCE: grows wild in southern India and Cechin-China; now cultivated in the East and West Indies, Malay Archipelago, the Philippines, Java, Sumatra and Borneo.
PARTS USED: the dried unripe fruits. White pepper comes from the same plant, except that the pericarp of the fruit has been removed prior to drying. The active chemicals in black or white pepper are piperine, volatile oil, starch, cellulose and a resin that is called chavicin.
MEDICINAL USES: aromatic, stimulant, carminative, febrifuge.

The herb is useful in treating constipation, gonorrhoea, prolapsed rectum, paralysis of the tongue and acts on the urinary organs. The stimulant properties of pepper work on the gastro-intestinal system to aid digestion, ease dyspepsia, torbid stomach conditions, and relieve flatulence and nausea. Pepper has also been recommended in diarrhoea, cholera, scarlatina, vertigo and paralytic and arthritic disorders. Peppercorns, as the dried fruit is known, are used both whole and ground in many culinary dishes and are used as a condiment. In the Siege of Rome in AD 408, pepper was so highly priced that it was used as a form of currency.

ADMINISTERED AS: powdered dried fruits, gargle.

Peppermint *Mentha piperita*.
COMMON NAME: brandy mint, curled mint, balm mint.
OCCURRENCE: found across Europe, was introduced into Britain and grows widely in damp places and waste ground.
PARTS USED: the herb and distilled oil. The plant contains peppermint oil, which is composed of menthol, menthyl acetate and isovalerate, menthone, cineol, pinene and limonene. The medicinal qualities are found in the alcoholic chemicals.
MEDICINAL USES: stimulant, antispasmodic, carminative, stomachic, oil of peppermint is extensively used in both medicine and commerce. It is good in dyspepsia, flatulence, colic and abdominal cramps. The oil allays sickness and nausea, is used for chorea and diarrhoea but is normally

used with other medicines to disguise unpalatable tastes and effects. Peppermint water is in most general use and is used to raise body temperature and induce perspiration. Peppermint tea can help ward off colds and influenza at an early stage, can calm heart palpitations and is used to reduce the appetite.

ADMINISTERED AS: infusion, distilled water, spirit, essential oil and fluid extract.

Pine oils – Siberian pine oil, from *Abies sibirica*; Pumilio pine oil, from *Pinus muge*; Sylvestris pine oil, from *Pinus sylvestris*.
PARTS USED: the oil produced when pine wood is distilled using steam under pressure.
MEDICINAL USES: rubefacient, aromatic. These oils are mainly used as inhalants for bronchitis or laryngitis or as liniment plasters.
ADMINISTERED AS: distilled oil.

Poppy, Red *Papaver rhoeas*.
COMMON NAME: headache, corn poppy, corn rose, *Flores rhoeados*.
OCCURRENCE: a common flowering plant in fields and waste ground across Europe and Great Britain.
PARTS USED: flowers and petals. The fresh petals contain rhoeadic and papaveric acids, which give the flowers their colour, and the alkaloid rhoeadine. The amount and quality of active ingredients in the plant are uncertain so its action is open to debate.

MEDICINAL USES: very slightly narcotic, anodyne, expectorant. The petals can be made into a syrup that is used to ease pain. It may be used for chest complaints, e.g. pleurisy.
ADMINISTERED AS: syrup, infusion, distilled water.

Poppy, White *Papaver somniferum.*
COMMON NAME: opium poppy, mawseed.
OCCURRENCE: indigenous to Turkey and Asia, cultivated in Europe, Great Britain, Persia, India and China for opium production.
PARTS USED: the capsules and flowers. The white poppy contains 21 different alkaloids, of which morphine, narcotine, codeine, codamine and thebaine are the most important.
MEDICINAL USES: hypnotic, sedative, astringent, expectorant, diaphoretic, antispasmodic, anodyne. Its use dates back to Greek and Roman times. It is the best possible hypnotic and sedative drug, frequently used to relieve pain and calm excitement. It has also been used in diarrhoea, dysentery and some forms of cough. The tincture of opium is commonly called laudanum, and when applied externally with soap liniment it provides quick pain relief.
ADMINISTERED AS: syrup, tincture, decoction and poultice.

Primrose *Primula vulgaris.*
OCCURRENCE: a common wild flower found in woods, hedgerows and pastures throughout Great Britain.
PARTS USED: the root and whole herb. Both parts of the plant

contain a fragrant oil called primulin and the active principle saponin.

MEDICINAL USES: astringent, antispasmodic, vermifuge, emetic. It was formerly considered to be an important remedy in muscular rheumatism, paralysis and gout. A tincture of the whole plant has sedative effects and is used successfully in extreme sensitivity, restlessness and insomnia. Nervous headaches can be eased by treatment with an infusion of the root, while the powdered dry root serves as an emetic. An infusion of primrose flowers is excellent in nervous headaches, and an ointment can be made out of the leaves to heal and salve wounds and cuts.

ADMINISTERED AS: infusion, tincture, powdered root and ointment.

Quince *Cydonia oblongata*.
COMMON NAME: quince seed, *Cydonica vulgaris*.
OCCURRENCE: grown in England for its fruit but is native to Persia.
PARTS USED: the fruit and seeds.
MEDICINAL USES: astringent, mucilaginous, demulcent. The fruit is used to prepare a syrup that is added to drinks when ill, as it restrains looseness of the bowels and helps relieve dysentery and diarrhoea. The soaked seeds form a mucilaginous mass similar to that produced by flax. A decoction of the seeds is used against gonorrhoea, thrush and in irritable conditions of the mucous membranes. The

liquid is also used as a skin lotion or cream and administered in eye diseases as a soothing lotion.

ADMINISTERED AS: syrup, decoction or lotion.

Rosemary *Rosmarinus officinalis*.

COMMON NAME: polar plant, compass weed, compass plant, romero, *Rosmarinus coronarium*.

OCCURRENCE: native to the dry hills of the Mediterranean, from Spain eastwards to Turkey. A common garden plant in Britain, having been cultivated prior to the Norman Conquest.

PARTS USED: the herb and root. Oil of rosemary is distilled from the plant tops and used medicinally. Rosemary contains tannic acid, a bitter principle, resin and a volatile oil.

MEDICINAL USES: tonic, astringent, diaphoretic, stimulant. The essential oil is also stomachic, nervine and carminative and cures many types of headache. It is mainly applied externally as a hair lotion that is said to prevent baldness and the formation of dandruff. The oil is used externally as a rubefacient and is added to liniments for fragrance and stimulant properties. Rosemary tea can remove headache, colic, colds and nervous diseases and may also lift nervous depression.

ADMINISTERED AS: infusion, essential oil and lotion.

Rowan tree *Pyrus aucuparia*.

COMMON NAME: mountain ash, *Sorbus aucuparia*, *Mespilus aucuparia*.

OCCURRENCE: generally distributed over Great Britain and Europe, especially at high altitudes.

PARTS USED: the bark and fruit. The fruit may contain tartaric, citric or malic acids, dependent on its stage of ripeness. It also contains sorbitol, sorbin, sorbit, parascorbic acid and bitter, acrid colouring matters. The bark contains amygdalin.

MEDICINAL USES: astringent, antiscorbutic. A decoction of rowan bark is given for diarrhoea and as a vaginal injection for leucorrhoea. The berries are made into an acid gargle to ease sore throats and inflamed tonsils. An infusion of the fruit is administered to ease haemorrhoids. The berries may also be made into jelly, flour, cider, ale or an alcoholic spirit. The rowan tree planted next to a house was said to protect the house against witchcraft.

ADMINISTERED AS: decoction, injection, infusion and dietary item.

Rue *Ruta graveolens.*

COMMON NAME: herb of grace, garden rue, herbygrass, ave-grace.

OCCURRENCE: indigenous to southern Europe and was introduced into Great Britain by the Romans.

PARTS USED: the herb. The herb is covered by glands that contain a volatile oil. The oil is composed of limonene, cineole, a crystalline substance called rutin and several acids. The plant also contains several alkaloids, including fagarine and arborinine as well as coumarins.

MEDICINAL USES: stimulant, antispasmodic, emmenagogue,

irritant, rubefacient. This is a very powerful herb and the dose administered should be kept low. It is useful in treating coughs, croup, colic, flatulence and hysteria, and it is particularly good against strained eyes and headaches caused by eyestrain. An infusion of the herb is good for nervous indigestion, heart palpitations, nervous headaches and to expel worms. The chemical rutin strengthens weak blood vessels and aids varicose veins. In Chinese medicine, rue is a specific for insect and snake bites. When made into an ointment, rue is effective in gouty and rheumatic pains, sprained and bruised tendons and chilblains. The bruised leaves irritate and blister the skin and so can ease sciatica. This herb should not be used in pregnancy as the volatile oil, alkaloids and coumarins in the plant all stimulate the uterus and strongly promote menstrual bleeding. When a fresh leaf is chewed, it flavours the mouth and relieves headache, giddiness or any hysterical spasms quickly.

ADMINISTERED AS: fresh leaf, volatile oil, ointment, infusion, decoction, tea, expressed juice.

Saffron *Crocus sativus*.

COMMON NAME: croccus, karcom, Alicante saffron, Valencia saffron, krokos, gatinais, saffron, hay saffron, saffron crocus.

OCCURRENCE: grown from Persia and Kurdistan in the east to most European countries, including Great Britain.

PARTS USED: the dried flower pistils. These parts contain an essential oil composed of terpenes, terepene alcohols and esters, a coloured glycoside called crocin and a bitter glucoside called picrocrocin.

MEDICINAL USES: carminative, diaphoretic, emmenagogue. This herb is used as a diaphoretic drug for children and can also help absent or painful menstruation and stop chronic haemorrhage of the uterus in adults.

ADMINISTERED AS: tincture, powdered saffron.

Sage, Common *Salvia officinalis.*
COMMON NAME: garden sage, red sage, saurge, broad-leaved white sage, *Salvia salvatrix.*
OCCURRENCE: native to the northern Mediterranean and cultivated through Britain, France and Germany.
PARTS USED: the leaves, whole herb. The herb contains a volatile oil, tannin and resin and is distilled to produce sage oil. This is made up of salvene, pinene, cineol, vorneol, thujone and some esters.
MEDICINAL USES: stimulant, astringent, tonic, carminative, aromatic. Sage makes an excellent gargle for relaxed throat and tonsils, bleeding gums, laryngitis and ulcerated throat. Sage tea is valuable against delirium of fevers, nervous excitement and accompanying brain and nervous diseases; as a stimulant tonic in stomach and nervous system complaints and in weak digestion. It also works as an emmenagogue in treating typhoid fever, bilious and liver problems, kidney troubles and lung or stomach haemorrhages. The infusion is used in head colds, quinsy, mea-

sles, painful joints, lethargy, palsy and nervous headaches. Fresh leaves are rubbed on the teeth to cleanse them and strengthen gums – even today sage is included in tooth powders. The oil of sage was used to remove mucus collections from the respiratory organs and it is included in embrocations for rheumatism. The herb is also applied warm as a poultice.

ADMINISTERED AS: infusion, essential oil, tea and poultice.

Salep: Early purple orchid *Orchis mascula*; Spotted orchid *Orchis maculata*; Marsh orchid *Orchis latifolia*.

COMMON NAME: saloop, schlep, satrion, Levant salep.

OCCURRENCE: *Orchis mascula* is found in woods throughout England. *O. maculata* grows wild on heaths and commons; *O. latifolia* is found growing in marshes and damp pastures across Great Britain.

PARTS USED: the tuberous root, which contains mucilage, sugar, starch and volatile oil.

MEDICINAL USES: very nutritive, demulcent. This herb is used as a food item for convalescent people and children, made with milk or water and flavoured. It is prepared in a similar way to ARROWROOT. A decoction with sugar, spice or wine was given to invalids to build them up. The root is used to stop irritation of the gastro-intestinal canal and for invalids suffering from bilious fevers or chronic diarrhoea. In the old sailing ships, salep was carried and used as an emergency food source. It was sold on street corners in London as a hot drink before coffee replaced its use as a beverage.

ADMINISTERED AS: decoction, dietary item.

Sandalwood *Santalum album*.

COMMON NAME: santalwood, sanders-wood.

OCCURRENCE: a tree native to India and the Malay Archipelago.

PARTS USED: the wood oil.

MEDICINAL USES: aromatic, antiseptic, diuretic. The oil is given internally for chronic mucous conditions, e.g. bronchitis, inflammation of the bladder. It is also used in chronic cystitis, gleet and gonorrhoea. The oil is used in aromatherapy to lessen tension and anxiety, and it was also considered a sexual stimulant in folk traditions. The fluid extract of sandalwood may be better tolerated by some people than the oil.

ADMINISTERED AS: wood oil, fluid extract.

Savory, Summer *Saturcia hortensis*.

COMMON NAME: garden savory.

OCCURRENCE: a shrub native to the Mediterranean region and introduced into Great Britain.

PARTS USED: the herb.

MEDICINAL USES: aromatic, carminative. This herb is mainly used in cookery as a pot herb or flavouring. In medicine, it is added to remedies to flavour and to add warmth. It was formerly used for colic and flatulence and was considered a good expectorant. A sprig of summer savory rubbed on a wasp or bee sting relieves the pain quickly.

ADMINISTERED AS: fresh or dried herb.

Senna, Alexandrian *Cassia acutifolia*; East Indian Senna *Cassia angustifolia*.

COMMON NAME: Nubian senna, Egyptian senna, tinnevelly senna, *Cassia senna, C. lenitiva, C. lanceolata, C. officinalis, C. aethiopica, Senna acutifolia*.

OCCURRENCE: *Cassia acutifolia* is native to the upper and middle Nile in Egypt and Sudan. *C. angustifolia* is indigenous to southern Arabia and is cultivated in southern and eastern India.

PARTS USED: the dried leaflets and pods. The active principles of senna can be extracted using water or dilute alcohol. The drug contains anthraquinone derivatives and their glucosides as well as cathartic acid as its active chemicals.

MEDICINAL USES: laxative, purgative, cathartic. This drug acts primarily on the lower bowel, acts locally upon the intestinal wall, increasing the peristaltic movements of the colon. The taste is nauseating and liable to cause sickness and griping pains. It is generally combined with aromatics, e.g. ginger or cinnamon, and stimulants to modify senna's deleterious effects. Generally, senna is a good medicine for children, people of a delicate constitution and elderly people. Senna pods have milder effects than the leaves and lack their griping effects.

ADMINISTERED AS: infusion, powdered leaves, syrup, fluid extract, tincture, dried pods.

Shepherd's purse *Capsella bursa-pastoris*.

COMMON NAME: shepherd's bag, shepherd's scrip, lady's purse, witches' pouches, case-weed, pick-pocket, blindweed, pepper and salt, sanguinary, mother's heart, poor man's parmacettie, clappe-de-pouch.

OCCURRENCE: native to Europe and found all over the world outside tropical zones.

PARTS USED: the whole plant, which contains various chemicals that have not yet been entirely analysed but include an organic acid, a volatile oil, a fixed oil, a tannate, an alkaloid and a resin.

MEDICINAL USES: haemostatic, antiscorbutic, diuretic, stimulant. As an infusion of the dried plant, shepherd's purse is one of the best specifics for arresting bleeding of all kinds, particularly from the kidneys, uterus, stomach or lungs. It is said to be as effective as ergot or golden seal. It has been used for diarrhoea, haemorrhoids, dysentery, dropsy and kidney complaints. Shepherd's purse is an important remedy in catarrhal infections of the bladder and ureter and in ulcerated and abscess of the bladder where it increases the flow of urine and provides relief. Externally, the bruised herb is used as a poultice on bruised and strained areas, rheumatic joints and for some skin problems. Since the herb tastes slightly unpleasant, it is normally taken internally with other herbs to disguise the flavour, e.g. couch grass, juniper, pellitory-of-the-wall.

ADMINISTERED AS: fluid extract, poultice, decoction, infusion.

Solomon's seal *Polygonatum multiflorum*.

COMMON NAME: lady's seals, St Mary's seal, *Sigillum sanctae Mariae*.

OCCURRENCE: a native plant of northern Europe and Siberia. It is found wild in some localities in England but naturalised in Scotland and Ireland.

PARTS USED: the rhizome, which contains asparagin, gum, sugar, starch, pectin and convallarin, one of the active chemicals in LILY OF THE VALLEY.

MEDICINAL USES: astringent, demulcent, tonic. When combined with other herbs, it is good for bleeding of the lungs and pulmonary complaints. It is used on its own in female complaints and as a poultice for tumours, inflammations, bruises and haemorrhoids. As it is mucilaginous, it makes a very good healing and restorative tonic for inflammation of the bowels and stomach, haemorrhoids and chronic dysentery. A decoction was used to cure erysipelas and was taken by people with broken bones, as Solomon's seal was supposed to 'encourage the bones to knit'. A distilled water prepared from the root was used as a cosmetic to remove spots, freckles and marks from the skin.

ADMINISTERED AS: decoction, infusion, poultice, distilled water.

Spearmint *Mentha viridis*.

COMMON NAME: mackerel mint, Our Lady's mint, green mint, spire mint, sage of Bethlehem, fish mint, lamb mint, menthe de Notre Dame, erba Santa Maria, *Mentha spicata*, *M. crispa*, yerba buena.

OCCURRENCE: originally a Mediterranean native and introduced into the British Isles by the Romans.

PARTS USED: the herb and essential oil. The main component of the essential oil is carvone along with phellandrine, limonene and dihydrocarveol acetate. The oil also has the esters of acetic, butyric and caproic acids within it.

MEDICINAL USES: antispasmodic, aromatic, carminative, stimulant. This herb is very similar to PEPPERMINT but it seems to be less powerful. It is more suited to children's remedies. A distilled water from spearmint is used to relieve hiccups, flatulence and indigestion, while the infusion is good for fevers, inflammatory diseases and all infantile troubles. Spearmint is considered a specific in stopping nausea and vomiting and in easing the pain caused by colic. As a homeopathic remedy, spearmint has been used for strangury, gravel and as a local application for painful haemorrhoids.

ADMINISTERED AS: distilled water, infusion, tincture, fluid extract.

St John's wort *Hypericum perforatum*.

OCCURRENCE: found in woods, hedges, roadsides and meadows across Britain, Europe and Asia.

PARTS USED: the herb and flowers.

MEDICINAL USES: aromatic, astringent, resolvent, expectorant, diuretic and nervine. It is generally utilised in all pulmonary complaints, bladder trouble, suppression of urine, dysentery, diarrhoea and jaundice. It is good against hysteria, nervous depression, haemorrhages, coughing up blood and dispelling worms from the body. If children have a problem with night incontinence, an infusion of St John's wort taken before bed will stop the problem. The herb is used externally to break up hard tissues, e.g. tumours, bruising and swollen, hard breasts when feeding infants.

ADMINISTERED AS: an infusion and poultice.

Sundew *Drosera rotundifolia.*

COMMON NAME: round-leaved sundew, dew plant, red rot, youth-wort, rosa solis, herba rosellae, rosée du soleil.

OCCURRENCE: an insectivorous plant found in bogs, wet places and river edges throughout Britain, Europe, India, China, North and South America and Russian Asia.

PARTS USED: the air-dried flowering plant.

MEDICINAL USES: pectoral, expectorant, demulcent, anti-asthmatic. In small doses sundew is a specific in dry, spasmodic, tickling coughs and is considered very good in whooping cough, for which it may also be used as a prophylactic drug. The fresh juice is used to remove corns and warts. In America, the sundew has been advocated as a cure for old age and has been used with colloidal silicates in cases of the thickening of arteries caused by old age or calcium or fat deposition.

ADMINISTERED AS: fluid extract, expressed juice, solid extract.

Sunflower *Helicanthus annuus*.

COMMON NAME: helianthus, marigold of Peru, *Sola indianus*, *Chrysanthemum peruvianum*, *Corona solis*.

OCCURRENCE: native to Peru and Mexico and was introduced into America, Europe and Great Britain as a garden plant.

PARTS USED: the seeds. These contain a vegetable oil, carbonate of potash, tannin and vitamins B_1, B_3 and B_6. The oil is expressed from the crushed seeds and, according to the range of temperature to which the seeds are heated, several grades of oil are obtained.

MEDICINAL USES: diuretic, expectorant. It has been used successfully in treating pulmonary, bronchial and laryngeal afflictions as well as whooping cough, colds and coughs. The leaves are used in some parts of the world to treat malaria, and the tincture may replace quinine in easing intermittent fevers and the ague. Sunflowers produce the seed cake that is used as cattle food; the fresh leaves are given to poultry; the plants can be used as a vegetable; the stems are used as bedding for ducks; the plant used for silage, fuel, manure and textiles.

ADMINISTERED AS: sunflower oil, tincture, decoction, poultice.

Tarragon *Artemisia dracunculus*.

COMMON NAME: mugwort, little dragon.

OCCURRENCE: cultivated in kitchen gardens across Europe and Great Britain. Tarragon originally arose from both Siberia and southern Europe to form the French and Russian tarragon we know today.

PARTS USED: the leaves, which contain an essential volatile oil that is lost on drying.

MEDICINAL USES: today there are few medicinal uses for tarragon but it has been used previously to stimulate the appetite and to cure toothache. Tarragon is mostly used in cooking - particularly on the European continent. It is used for dressings, salads, vinegar and pickles.

ADMINISTERED AS: fresh root, fresh herb.

Tea *Camellia thea*.

COMMON NAME: Camellia theifera, Thea sinensis, T. veridis, T. bohea, T. stricta jassamica.

OCCURRENCE: native to Assam in India, and the plant has spread to Sri Lanka, Java, China and Japan.

PARTS USED: the dried leaves.

MEDICINAL USES: stimulant, astringent. The infusion of the leaves has a stimulating effect on the nervous system, producing a feeling of comfort. It may also act as a nerve sedative where it can relieve headaches. When drunk in excessive quantities, tea can produce unpleasant nervous symptoms, dyspepsia and unnatural wakefulness.

ADMINISTERED AS: infusion.

Thyme *Thymus vulgaris*.

COMMON NAME: garden or common thyme, tomillo.

OCCURRENCE: cultivated in temperate countries in northern Europe.

PARTS USED: the herb. Thyme gives rise to oil of thyme after distillation of the fresh leaves. This oil contains the phenols thymol and carvacrol as well as cymene, pinene and borneol.

MEDICINAL USES: antiseptic, antispasmodic, tonic, carminative. The fresh herb, in syrup, forms a safe cure for whooping cough, as is an infusion of the dried herb. The infusion or tea is beneficial for catarrh, sore throat, wind spasms, colic and in allaying fevers and colds. Thyme is generally used in conjunction with other remedies in herbal medicine.

ADMINISTERED AS: fluid extract, essential oil and infusion.

Turpentine oil distilled from *Pinus palustris*, *Pinus maritima* and other species.

MEDICINAL USES: rubefacient, irritant, diuretic. When taken internally, turpentine forms a valuable remedy in bladder, kidney, and rheumatic problems and diseases of the mucous membranes. The oil is also used for respiratory complaints and externally as a liniment, an embrocation and an inhalant for rheumatism and chest problems. Turpentine may be combined with other aromatic oils as a remedy.

ADMINISTERED AS: essential oil.

Valerian *Valeriana officinalis*.

COMMON NAME: all-heal, great wild valerian, amantilla, setwall, sete-wale, capon's tail.

OCCURRENCE: found throughout Europe and northern Asia. It is common in England in marshy thickets, riverbanks and ditches.

PARTS USED: the root, which contains a volatile oil, two alkaloids, called chatarine and valerianine, as well as several unidentified compounds.

MEDICINAL USES: powerful nervine, stimulant, carminative, anodyne and antispasmodic herb. It may be given in all cases of nervous debility and irritation as it is not narcotic. The expressed juice of the fresh root has been used as a narcotic in insomnia and as an anticonvulsant in epilepsy. The oil of valerian is of use against cholera and in strengthening the eyesight. A herbal compound containing valerian was given to civilians during the Second World War to reduce the effects of stress caused by repeated air raids and to minimise damage to health.

ADMINISTERED AS: fluid and solid extract, tincture, oil, expressed juice.

Violet *Viola adorata*.
COMMON NAME: blue violet, sweet violet, sweet-scented violet.
OCCURRENCE: native to Great Britain and found widely over Europe, northern Asia and North America.
PARTS USED: the dried flowers and leaves and whole plant when fresh.
MEDICINAL USES: antiseptic, expectorant, laxative. The herb is mainly taken as syrup of violets, which has been used to

cure the ague, epilepsy, eye inflammation, pleurisy, jaundice and sleeplessness that are some of the many other complaints that benefit from treatment with this herb. The flowers possess expectorant properties and have long been used to treat coughs. The flowers may also be crystallised as a sweetmeat or added to salads. The rhizome is strongly emetic and purgative and has violent effects when administered. The seeds also have purgative and diuretic effects and are beneficial in treating urinary complaints and gravel. In the early part of this century, violet preparations were used to great effect against cancer. Fresh violet leaves are made into an infusion that was drunk regularly, and a poultice of the leaves was applied to the affected area. The herb has been used successfully to both allay pain and perhaps cure the cancer. It is said to be particularly good against throat cancer. ADMINISTERED AS: infusion, poultice, injection, ointment, syrup and powdered root.

Walnut *Juglans nigra*.
COMMON NAME: carya, Jupiter's nuts, *Juglans regia*.
OCCURRENCE: cultivated throughout Europe and probably native to Persia.
PARTS USED: the bark and leaves. The active principle of the walnut tree is nucin, or juglon, while the kernels also contain oil, mucilage, albumin, cellulose, mineral matter and water.
MEDICINAL USES: alterative, laxative, detergent, astringent. The bark and leaves are used in skin problems, e.g. scrofulous

diseases, herpes, eczema and for healing indolent ulcers. A strong infusion of the powdered bark has purgative effects, while the walnut has various properties dependent on its stage of ripeness. Green walnuts are anthelminthic and vermifuge in action and are pickled in vinegar that is then used as a gargle for sore and ulcerated throats. The wood is used for furniture, gunstocks and for cabinets. Walnut oil expressed from the kernels is used in wood polishing and in painting and is used as butter or frying oil.

ADMINISTERED AS: fluid extract, infusion, expressed oil, whole fruit.

Water dock *Rumex aquaticus.*
COMMON NAME: red dock, bloodwort.
OCCURRENCE: found frequently in fields, meadows, pools and ditches throughout Europe and Great Britain and is particularly common in the northern latitudes.
PARTS USED: the root.
MEDICINAL USES: alterative, deobstruent, detergent. It has a tonic action and is used externally to clean ulcers in afflictions of the mouth. It is applied to eruptive and scorbutic diseases, skin ulcers and sores. As a powder, water dock has a cleansing and detergent effect upon the teeth.
ADMINISTERED AS: fluid extract and infusion.

Watercress *Nasturtium officinale.*
OCCURRENCE: a perennial creeping plant often growing near springs and running water across Great Britain and Europe.

PARTS USED: the stem and leaves, which contain nicotinamide, volatile oil, a glucoside, gluconasturtin and vitamins A, C and E.

MEDICINAL USES: stimulant, expectorant, nutritive, antiscorbutic, diuretic. Watercress was proposed as a specific in tuberculosis and has a very long history of medical use. It is used to treat bronchitis and coughs as well as boosting digestion, lowering blood sugar and helping the body to remove toxic wastes from the blood and tissues. The herb is of value nutritionally as it contains many vitamins and mineral salts that help during convalescence and general debility. It can be bruised and made into a poultice for arthritis and gout, and is chewed raw to strengthen gums.

ADMINISTERED AS: expressed juice, poultice, dietary item.

Wintergreen *Gaultheria procumbens.*

COMMON NAME: mountain tea, teaberry, boxberry, thé du Canada, aromatic wintergreen, partridge berry, deerberry, checkerberry.

OCCURRENCE: native to Canada and the northern United States from Georgia northwards.

PARTS USED: the leaves, which produce a volatile oil upon distillation. The oil is made up of methyl salicylate, gaultherilene, an aldehyde, a secondary alcohol and an ester. The aromatic odour of the plant is the result of the alcohol and the ester.

MEDICINAL USES: aromatic, tonic, stimulant, diuretic,

emmenagogue, astringent, galactogogue. The oil is of great benefit in acute rheumatism but must be given in the form of capsules so stomach inflammation does not occur. The true distilled oil when applied to the skin can give rise to an eruption, so the synthetic oil of wintergreen is recommended for external use as it still contains methyl salicylate but with no deleterious effects. The synthetic oil is exceedingly valuable for all chronic joint and muscular troubles, lumbago, sciatica and rheumatism. The oil is also used as a flavouring for toothpowders and mouthwashes, particularly when combined with menthol and EUCALYPTUS. The berries are a winter food for many animals and also produce a bitter tonic after being steeped in brandy. The leaves are either used to flavour tea or as a substitute for tea itself.

ADMINISTERED AS: capsules, synthetic oil, infusion, tincture.

Woodruff *Asperula odorata*.
COMMON NAME: wuderove, wood-rova, sweet woodruff, woodroof, waldmeister tea.
OCCURRENCE: grows in woods or shaded hedges in England.
PARTS USED: the herb, which contains coumarin, a fragrant crystalline chemical, citric, malic and rubichloric acids and tannic acid.
MEDICINAL USES: diuretic, tonic. The fresh leaves, when applied to wounds, were said to have a strong healing effect. A strong decoction of the fresh herb was used as a cordial

and stomachic and is said to be useful in removing biliary obstructions of the liver.

ADMINISTERED AS: a poultice and decoction.

Wormwood *Artemisia absinthium*.

COMMON NAME: green ginger, old women, ajenjo.

OCCURRENCE: a plant found wild in many parts of the world, including Siberia, Europe and the United States of America.

PARTS USED: the whole herb. The herb contains a volatile oil made up of thujone, pinene, cadinene and chamazulene, a bitter principle called absinthum, carotene, tannins and vitamin C.

MEDICINAL USES: bitter tonic, anthelmintic, febrifuge, stomachic. The liqueur, absinthe, was made using this plant as flavouring and it was banned in France in 1915 as excess intake caused irreversible damage to the nervous system. In modern herbal medicine, it is used as a bitter tonic to stimulate the appetite, the liver and gall bladder, production of digestive juices and peristalsis. Wormwood also expels parasitic worms, particularly roundworms and threadworms. The plant contains chemicals that have anti-inflammatory effects and help reduce fevers. Since ancient times this herb has been used by women to encourage menstruation, and it is applied as an external compress during labour to speed up the birth process. After labour, wormwood was taken both internally and externally to expel the afterbirth. This herb should not be used during pregnancy and should only be administered for short periods.

ADMINISTERED AS: infusion, essential oil, fluid extract.

Woundwort *Stachys palustris.*
COMMON NAME: all-heal, panay, opopanewort, clown's woundwort, rusticum vulna herba, downy woundwort, stinking marsh stachys.
OCCURRENCE: common to marshy meadows, riversides and ditches in most parts of Great Britain.
PARTS USED: the herb.
MEDICINAL USES: antiseptic, antispasmodic. The herb relieves cramp, gout, painful joints and vertigo, while bruised leaves will stop bleeding and encourage healing when applied to a wound. Woundwort had an excellent reputation as a vulnerary among all the early herbalists. A syrup made of the fresh juice will stop haemorrhages and dysentery when taken internally. The tuberous roots are edible, as are the young shoots, which resemble asparagus.
ADMINISTERED AS: poultice or syrup.

Yam, Wild *Dioscorea villosa.*
COMMON NAME: dioscorea, colic root, rheumatism root, wilde yamwurzel.
OCCURRENCE: native to the southern United States and Canada.
PARTS USED: the roots and rhizome, which contain steroidal

saponins, phytosterols, tannins, starch and various alkaloids, including dioscorine.

MEDICINAL USES: antispasmodic, diuretic. This plant has a history of traditional use in relieving menstrual cramps and in stopping threatened miscarriage. It brings quick relief for bilious colic and flatulence, particularly in pregnant women. It is prescribed for the inflammatory stage of rheumatoid arthritis and in painful disorders of the urinary tract. Wild yam is also beneficial for poor circulation, spasmodic hiccups, neuralgic complaints and spasmodic asthma. Prior to 1970, the wild yam was the only source of diosgenin, one of the starting materials used in commercial manufacturing of steroid hormones for the contraceptive pill.

ADMINISTERED AS: fluid extract, powdered bark, infusion.

Yew *Taxus baccata*.

OCCURRENCE: found in Europe, North Africa and western Asia. The tree has been closely associated with the history and legends of Europe.

PARTS USED: the leaves, seeds and fruit. The seeds and fruit are the most poisonous parts of the plant and contain an alkaloid toxin and another principle, milrossin.

MEDICINAL USES: it has few medicinal uses because of its poisonous nature, but the leaves were once used effectively in treating epilepsy. The wood was used for making longbows.

ADMINISTERED AS: powdered leaves.

Herb action

alterative   a term given to a substance that speeds up the renewal of the tissues so that they can carry out their functions more effectively.

anodyne   a drug that eases and soothes pain.

anthelmintic   a substance that causes the death or expulsion of parasitic worms.

antiperiodic   a drug that prevents the return of recurring diseases, e.g. malaria.

antiscorbutic   a substance that prevents scurvy and contains necessary vitamins, e.g. vitamin C.

antiseptic   a substance that prevents the growth of disease-causing microorganisms, e.g. bacteria, without causing damage to living tissue. It is applied to wounds to cleanse them and prevent infection.

antispasmodic a drug that diminishes muscle spasms.

aperient   a medicine that produces a natural movement of the bowel.

aphrodisiac   a compound that excites the sexual organs.

aromatic a   substance that has an aroma.

astringent   a substance that causes cells to contract by losing proteins from their surface. This causes localised contraction of blood vessels and tissues.

balsamic	a substance that contains resins and benzoic acid and is used to alleviate colds and abrasions.
bitter	a drug that is bitter-tasting and is used to stimulate the appetite.
cardiac	compounds that have some effect on the heart.
carminative	a preparation to relieve flatulence and any resultant griping.
cathartic	a compound that produces an evacuation of the bowels.
cholagogue	the name given to a substance that produces a flow of bile from the gall bladder.
cooling	a substance that reduces the temperature and cools the skin.
demulcent	a substance that soothes and protects the alimentary canal.
deobstruent	a compound that is said to clear obstructions and open the natural passages of the body.
detergent	a substance that has a cleansing action, either internally or on the skin.
diaphoretic	a term given to drugs that promote perspiration.
diuretics	a substance that stimulates the kidneys and increases urine and solute production.

emetic	a drug that induces vomiting.
emmenagogue	a compound that is able to excite the menstrual discharge.
emollient	a substance that softens or soothes the skin.
expectorant	a group of drugs that are taken to help in the removal of secretions from the lungs, bronchi and trachea.
febrifuge	a substance that reduces fever.
galactogogue	an agent that stimulates the production of breast milk or increases milk flow.
haemostatic	a drug used to control bleeding.
hepatic	a substance that acts upon the liver.
hydrogogue	a substance that has the property of removing accumulations of water or serum.
hypnotic	a drug or substance that induces sleep.
insecticide	a substance that kills insects.
irritant	a general term encompassing any agent that causes irritation of a tissue.
laxative	a substance that is taken to evacuate the bowel or soften stools.
mydriatic	a compound that causes dilation of the pupil.
nervine	a name given to drugs that are used to restore the nerves to their natural state.
narcotic	a drug that leads to a stupor and total loss of awareness.

nephritic	a drug that has an action on the kidneys.
nutritive	a compound that is nourishing to the body.
parasiticide	a substance that destroys parasites internally and externally.
pectoral	a term applied to drugs that are remedies in treating chest and lung complaints.
purgative	the name given to drugs or other measures that produce evacuation of the bowels. They normally have a more severe effect than aperients or laxatives.
refrigerant	a substance that relieves thirst and produces a feeling of coolness.
resolvent	a substance that is applied to swellings to reduce them in size.
rubefacient	a compound that causes the skin to redden and peel off. It causes blisters and inflammation.
sedative	a drug that lessens tension and anxiety and soothes over-excitement of the nervous system.
sternutatory	the name given to a substance that irritates the mucous membrane and produces sneezing.
stimulant	a drug or other agent that increases the activity of an organ or system within the body.

stomachic	a name given to drugs that treat stomach disorders.
styptic	applications that check bleeding by blood vessel contraction or by causing rapid blood-clotting.
sudorific	a drug or agent that produces copious perspiration.
taeniacide	drugs that are used to expel tapeworms from the body.
tonic	substances that are traditionally thought to give strength and vigour to the body and that are said to produce a feeling of wellbeing.
vermifuge	a substance that kills, or expels, worms from the intestines.
vesicant	similar to a rubefacient, agent that causes blistering when applied to the skin.
vulnerary	a drug that is said to be good at healing wounds.

Forms of herbal preparations

capsule
this is a gelatine container for swallowing and holding oils or balsams that would otherwise be difficult to administer because of their unpleasant taste or smell. It is used for cod liver oil and castor oil.

decoction
this is prepared using cut, bruised or ground bark and roots placed into a stainless steel or enamel pan (not aluminium) with cold water poured on. The mixture is boiled for 20–30 minutes, cooled and strained. It is best drunk when warm.

herbal dressing
this may be a compress or poultice. A compress is made of cloth or cotton wool soaked in cold or warm herbal decoctions or infusions while a poultice can be made with fresh or dried herbs. Bruised fresh herbs are applied directly to the affected area and dried herbs are made into a paste with water and placed on gauze on the required area. Both dressings are very effective in easing pain, swelling and inflammation of the skin and tissues.

infusion
this liquid is made from ground or bruised roots, bark, herbs or seeds, by pouring boiling water onto the herb and

leaving it to stand for 10-30 minutes, possibly stirring the mixture occasionally. The resultant liquid is strained and used. Cold infusions may be made if the active principles are yielded from the herb without heat. Today, infusions may be packaged into teabags for convenience.

liquid extract this preparation, if correctly made, is the most concentrated fluid form in which herbal drugs may be obtained and, as such, is very popular and convenient. Each herb is treated by various means dependent upon the individual properties of the herb, e.g. cold percolation, high pressure, evaporation by heat in a vacuum. These extracts are commonly held in a household stock of domestic remedies.

pessary similar to suppositories, but it is used in female complaints to apply a preparation to the walls of the vagina and cervix.

pill probably the best known and most widely used herbal preparation. It is normally composed of concentrated extracts and alkaloids, in combination with active crude drugs. The pill may be coated with sugar or another pleasant-tasting sub-

	stance that is readily soluble in the stomach.
solid extract	this type of preparation is prepared by evaporating the fresh juices or strong infusions of herbal drugs to the consistency of honey. It may also be prepared from an alcoholic tincture base. It is used mainly to produce pills, plasters, ointments and compressed tablets.
suppository	this preparation is a small cone of a convenient and easily soluble base with herbal extracts added, which is used to apply medicines to the rectum. It is very effective in the treatment of piles, cancers, etc.
tablet	this is made by compressing drugs into a small compass. It is more easily administered and has a quicker action as it dissolves more rapidly in the stomach.
tincture	this is the most prescribed form of herbal medicine. It is based on alcohol and, as such, removes certain active principles from herbs that will not dissolve in water, or in the presence of heat. The tincture produced is long-lasting, highly concentrated and needs to be taken only in small doses for beneficial effects. The ground

or chopped dried herb is placed in a container with 40 per cent alcohol such as gin or vodka and left for two weeks. The tincture is then decanted into a dark bottle and sealed before use.

Exercise

There is universal agreement among both conventional and alternative health practitioners about the benefits of regular exercise for promoting and maintaining good health. Naturopaths may recommend exercise for the relief of various disorders, and it is of known benefit in the treatment of constipation, hypertension and depression among other conditions. Exercise helps to prevent the heart and circulatory disorders that are so prevalent among people in Western countries. For all people, even those suffering from chronic disease, exercise within the limits of their strength makes them feel better and promotes healthy appetite and sleep. The benefits and forms of exercise are discussed in more detail below.

Regular physical exercise is vital throughout life to help maintain good health. Exercise burns up extra calories in food and reduces the likelihood of these being converted into fat. It confers a sense of wellbeing, improves appetite and sleep, and makes the heart and circulation, lungs and respiration work more efficiently. Exercise trains the heart so that the muscle fibres become stronger and pump a greater volume of blood with each beat. The result of this is that the resting heartbeat rate slows down and the system works more efficiently. This is achieved by fairly vigorous, regular exercise sufficient to raise the heart and respiration rate, carried out for about 20 minutes three times a week (or longer once a person becomes fit). Exercise helps to lower blood pressure through its beneficial effects on the heart and circulation, hence reducing the incidence of problems arising from this condition. It raises the basal metabolic rate, which means that the number of calories used while the body is at rest (for respiration, heartbeat, digestion, kidney and liver functions, etc) is increased. Once again, this means that there is less likelihood of gaining weight. Exercise, particularly some forms of weight-bearing activities, pumps calcium into bones and helps to maintain their density and strength. In older age, this has been shown to reduce significantly the rate at which bone density is lost, hence lessening the risk of fractures.

Different types of exercise and activity can improve bodily health in three main ways:

(1) Stamina, fitness or endurance is the ability to sustain a period of vigorous activity without having to stop because your heart is racing and you are gasping for breath. This is built up gradually by an exercise regime that improves the heart, circulation, lungs and respiration in the manner outlined above. An improvement in fitness is usually noticed quite quickly, after a few weeks of regular, fairly hard exercise, and provides great encouragement to continue. Unfortunately, however, the

level of fitness soon declines if the exercise regime is abandoned. Aerobic activities such as vigorous walking, jogging, cycling, dancing and fast swimming, along with many sports – football, tennis, squash, badminton etc – improve fitness.

(2) Flexibility is the ability of muscles and joints to perform their full range of movements – twisting, flexing and stretching – with suppleness and ease. There are many exercises that are designed to improve the flexibility and tone of various muscles and joints in different parts of the body, and numerous books on this subject. Health practitioners are usually happy to advise on the type of exercises that would be of greatest benefit to an individual patient. Such exercises, involving stretching, loosening up and bending, should also be performed before and after vigorous aerobic activities or sports in order to lessen the risk of injuries or cramps.

(3) Strength exercises are aimed at increasing the tone and sometimes the bulk of muscles, leading to the firming up of the body and an improvement in posture. The exercises and activities mentioned above play a part in this but so also do the use of weights, and specially designed equipment in a gym falls into this category. Certain medical conditions preclude the use of weights so it is best to check with a doctor before embarking upon this form of activity.

Most people recognise the need to undertake physical exercise, but for many a perceived lack of free time makes it difficult for them to fit this into their daily routine. People also commonly make the mistake of launching into a fast and vigorous form of exercise when they are not at all fit to do so. This can be dangerous if there is any underlying undiagnosed condition, such as heart disease, and may also be a cause of injury. In any exercise regime, it is important to be sensible and to increase the level of activity as and when fitness improves. People who are prepared to take a critical look at their daily routine usually find that there are places where they can fit in some physical exercise without unduly disrupting their schedule. A good, and often quoted, example of this is to use the stairs rather than the lift at work or to park the car farther away in order to fit in a brisk walk or run. It is important to realise that even small measures such as these have a beneficial effect and help to improve fitness, providing a base on which to progress to more vigorous forms of activity. Several routine home activities also fall into this category, e.g. cleaning the house, decorating and DIY, gardening and mowing the lawn, etc, because various muscles are being used and the person is actively moving about.

It is advisable for a person aged over 35 years or one who is overweight to have a medical checkup before embarking on any form of vigorous physical activity. With all exercise, it is vital to stop if anything becomes painful, very uncomfortable or if one is fighting for breath. Do not undertake hard exercise after eating a heavy meal. It is best to eat a starchy meal, which will provide plenty of energy, about three hours before beginning the activity and to drink plenty of water before, during and after the exercise period. Avoid physical activity if you have any form of illness, particularly if you are feverish or anaemic, and if you have a persistent medical condition exercise in accordance with medical advice. Always make sure that you are wearing the correct clothing, footwear and head gear appropriate for the activity and that it is of good quality and fits well. Injuries are often caused through neglect in this area and the cost of equipment is a factor that needs to be taken into account when planning an exercise programme.

Finally, it is very important to choose a form of physical exercise that you enjoy and that is appropriate for you. Although this may seem obvious, people can be influenced by many factors and do not always make wise choices. Of course, there is no harm in trying something to see if you like it but be prepared to give it up if you do not. You are far more likely to succeed in the activity, and hence improve your level of fitness, if you enjoy it and look forward to the times when you can carry it out.

Counselling and Lifestyle Modification

Introduction

A naturopath is interested in the person as a whole and not just in a particular condition or set of symptoms that may be troubling the patient. He or she will therefore take considerable time in talking to the patient and asking detailed questions about the person's background, employment, family, habits and lifestyle. Naturally, this is a two-way process and the patient is encouraged to talk about health and any other problems that may be proving troublesome. Apart from any specific treatment and dietary changes, the naturopath may suggest alterations in lifestyle, which could include matters like giving up smoking or alcohol, taking more exercise and advising on ways of managing stress. A programme of *relaxation exercises* may be suggested or the use of *visualisation (image) therapy*, *colour*, *music* or *dance therapy* or *hypnotherapy*, depending upon the individual circumstances.

Relaxation exercises

Relaxation exercises include the use of breathing to bring

about a change in the state of the body and mind. Usually, this involves becoming aware that the diaphragm should be involved in breathing as, too often, people in adult life rely on the chest and rib cage to force air into and out of the lungs. In chest breathing, the process is rapid and shallow, and the lungs fail to empty properly. It is the method of breathing that all people resort to at times of physical and psychological stress. However, if used continually it becomes a cause of stress in itself. The diaphragm is a membrane of muscle and tendon that separates the thoracic and abdominal cavities. The diaphragm bulges up to its resting position during exhalation, forcing air out of the lungs as it moves upwards into the chest cavity. During inspiration it flattens, thereby reducing pressure in the thoracic cavity and drawing air in to fill the lungs completely. This ensures that a good supply of oxygen enters the blood and tissues and the efficient elimination of carbon dioxide. It helps to lower blood pressure and directly relieves anxiety, tension and stress.

Relaxation exercises may take a number of different forms but a commonly used method is termed *progressive relaxation*. In this, the person lies on his or her back on a comfortable surface. Beginning with the head and face, groups of muscles are consciously contracted and 'held' for one or two minutes before being relaxed. The process proceeds downwards through the neck, shoulders, chest, arms, abdomen, legs and feet until all muscles are completely relaxed. A variation is to use thoughts to concentrate on the different areas to induce them to relax completely.

Visualisation therapy

It is now widely accepted that the mind exerts a great deal of influence on the health of the body. People with a cheerful, optimistic outlook on life often experience better health than those who are gloomy and pessimistic. In the case of some serious illnesses, such as cancer, it is recognised that people who maintain a positive and determined attitude often do better than those who are passive or fatalistic. In these instances, life in both its extent and quality appears to be affected by the person's state of mind. In visualisation therapy it is recognised that the pictures created by the mind (as well as thoughts) can have powerful positive or negative effects on the health of the body. Those using this technique believe that it not only helps people suffering from stress and psychological and emotional problems but also patients with physical illnesses and symptoms. These include cancer, rheumatic and arthritic disorders and other painful conditions.

In visualisation therapy, the patient is first taught the technique of creating a mental image. A person suffering from an emotional or psychological problem is asked to create a picture that is connected with his or her difficulty. The feelings created by the image are explored and discussed with the therapist and changes are made to the picture that, with time, help to resolve the problem. For people with physical illnesses, the image created is often aimed at helping to relieve and ease pain by creating an image of the diseased or painful area and making adjustments to it with the aim of reducing the impact of the symptoms. However, its benefits in the treatment of physical disorders remain controversial.

This form of treatment is normally used with other techniques. It is beneficial for people suffering from stress and emotional problems. Children often respond well to visualisation therapy as they are naturally imaginative and find it easy to create mental pictures.

Colour therapy

Colour therapy uses coloured light to treat disease and disorder and to help restore good heath. It is well known that human beings respond to coloured light and are affected in different ways by rays of various wavelengths. This even occurs in people who are blind, so the human body is able to respond in subtle ways to electromagnetic radiation. Colour therapists believe that each individual receives and absorbs electromagnetic radiation from the sun and emits it in a unique 'aura' – a pattern of colours peculiar to that person. It is believed that the aura can be recorded on film by a photographic technique known as *Kirlian photography*. If disease is present, this manifests itself as a disturbance of the vibrations that form the aura, giving a distorted pattern. During a consultation, a colour therapist pays particular attention to the patient's spine as each individual vertebra is believed to reflect the condition of a particular part of the body. Hence the aura from each vertebra is believed to indicate the health of its corresponding body part. Each vertebra is believed to be related to one of the eight colours of the visible spectrum. The eight colours are repeated in their usual sequence from the top to the base of the spine.

The treatment consists of bathing the body in coloured light, with appropriate colours being decided upon by the therapist. Usually one main colour is used along with a complementary one, and the light is emitted in irregular bursts. Treatment sessions last for a little less than 20 minutes and are continued for at least seven weeks. The aim is to restore the natural balance in the pattern of the aura. A therapist also advises on the use of colours in the home and of clothes and soft furnishings, etc.

In orthodox medicine it is accepted that colours exert subtle influences on people, especially affecting their state of mind and psychological wellbeing. Colour therapy may well aid healing, but there is no scientific evidence to explain the way in which this might work.

Dance movement therapy

Dance movement therapy is aimed at helping people to resolve deep-seated problems by communicating with, and relating to, others through the medium of physical movements and dance. The ability to express deep inner feelings in 'body language' and physical movements is innate in human beings. Young children express themselves freely in this way and without inhibition, and dancing would appear to be common to all past and present races and tribes of people. In modern industrial societies, however, many people find themselves unable to communicate their problems and fears either verbally or physically and may repress them to such an extent that they become ill. Dance movement therapy aims to help people to explore, recognise and come to terms with feelings and problems that they usually repress, and to communicate them to others. This therapy can help emotional, psychological and stress-related disorders, anxiety and depression, addiction, problems related to physical or sexual abuse, and learning disabilities. Children are often very responsive to this therapy and it may help those who have behavioural or intellectual problems, autism or other mental and physical disabilities.

People of any age can take part in dance movement therapy as the aim is to explore gently physical movements that are within each person's capabilities. The therapist may suggest movements, but hopes to encourage patients to learn to take the initiative. Eventually some groups learn to talk over feelings and problems that have emerged through taking part and are better able to resolve them.

Dance therapy sessions are organised in some hospitals and 'drop-in' and daycare centres. This form of therapy is regarded as particularly beneficial for people suffering from a number of disorders, particularly those with psychological and emotional problems or who are intellectually disadvantaged.

Hypnotherapy

The aim of hypnotherapy is that the patient and therapist work together to achieve a cure. There are a variety of disorders that have been treated with success, such as migraine, irritable bowel syndrome, ulcers and skin disorders, along with other problems caused by stress and anxiety. Illnesses known as hysterical illness are a relatively common problem that hypnotherapists treat. They include phobias (a fear of flying, heights, etc), insomnia and asthma. The pain of childbirth can also be relieved.

To induce a trance, a patient will be asked to concentrate his or her attention on a fixed object or something that is moving slowly, and this will encourage the patient to become drowsy. While the patient is at this level of consciousness, the therapist is able to encourage him or her to view any problem more positively, to realise what he or she can achieve and also to understand any events in his or her past history and how he or she might be likely to react in the future. It is quite unusual for a patient actually to go to sleep after having been in a trance. Should this happen, it demonstrates only that the person has not had sufficient sleep and is merely tired. It is quite commonplace for patients to use hypnosis on themselves after the ailment or problem, such as insomnia or asthma, has been resolved. With a little daily practice, they will be able to help themselves considerably should the need arise for further or frequent treatment. To assist the patient, a therapist might provide a prerecorded tape of the known commencement of each session which leads up to the trance.

Hypnotherapy can be beneficial in relieving pain and is valuable in the treatment of various psychosomatic disorders. A naturopath may be a qualified practitioner in this field or may be able to refer the patient to such a therapist if, after full discussion, it is agreed that hypnotherapy may prove helpful.

Naturopathic Therapies

Naturopaths may recommend the use of various therapies and may have their own particular speciality. These methods include:

Massage

As long ago as 3000 BC massage was used as a therapy in the Far East, making it one of the oldest treatments used by humans. In the year 5 BC in ancient Greece, Hippocrates recommended that to maintain health a massage using oils should be taken daily after a perfumed bath. Greek physicians were well used to treating people who suffered from pain and stiffness in the joints. The relaxation and healing powers of massage have been well documented over the past 5,000 years.

Massage increased in popularity when, in the 19th century, Per Henrik Ling, a Swedish fencing master and academic, created the basis for what is now known as *Swedish massage*. Swedish massage deals with the soft tissues of the body. It is a combination of relaxing effects and exercises that work on the joints and muscles, but it is still based on the form that was practised in ancient times. More recently, a work was published in the 1970s called *The Massage Book,* by George Downing, and this introduced a new concept in the overall technique of massage – that the whole person's state should be assessed by the therapist and not solely the physical side. The emotional and mental states should be part of the overall picture. Also combined in his form of massage were the methods used in reflexology and shiatsu, and this was known as *therapeutic massage*. The aim of this is to use relaxation, stimulation and invigoration to promote good health.

This massage is commonly used to induce general relaxation, so that any tension or strain experienced in the rush of daily life can be eased and eliminated. It is found to be very effective, working on the mind as well as the body. It can be used to treat people with hypertension (high blood pressure), sinusitis, headaches, insomnia and hyperactivity, including people who suffer from heart ailments or circulatory disorders. At the physical level, massage is intended to help the body make use of food and to eliminate the waste materials as well as stimulating the nervous and muscular system and the circulation of blood. Neck and back pain are conditions from which many people suffer, particularly if they have not been sitting correctly, such as in a slightly stooped position with their shoulders rounded. People whose day-to-day work involves a great deal of physical activity, such as dancers and athletes, can also derive a great deal of benefit from the use of massage. Stiffness can be a problem that they have after training or working, and this is relieved by encouraging the toxins that gather in the muscles to disperse.

Massage promotes a feeling of calmness and serenity, and this is particularly beneficial to people who frequently suffer from bouts of depression or anxiety. Once the worry and depression have been dispelled, people are able to deal with their problems much more effectively and, being able to do so, will boost their self-confidence.

In hospitals, massage has been used to ease pain and discomfort as well as being of benefit to people who are bedridden, since the flow of blood to the muscles is stimulated. It has also been used for those who have suffered a heart attack and has helped their recovery. A more recent development has been the use of massage for cancer patients who are suffering from the after-effects of treatment, such as chemotherapy, as well as the discomfort that the disease itself causes. Indeed, there are few conditions when it is not recommended. However, it should not be used when people are suffering from inflammation of the veins (phlebitis), varicose veins, thrombosis (clots in the blood) or if they have a raised temperature such as occurs during a fever. It is then advisable to contact a doctor before using massage.

It is quite usual nowadays for a masseur or masseuse to combine treatment with the use of other methods, such as aromatherapy, acupuncture or reflexology. Massage can be divided into four basic forms, and these are known as *percussion* (also known as *drumming* or *tapotement*); *friction* (also called *pressure*); *effleurage* (also called *stroking*) and *petrissage* (also called *kneading*). These four methods can be practised alone or in combination for maximum benefit to the patient. Massage is a therapy in which both parties derive an overall feeling of wellbeing – the therapist by the skilful use of the hands to impart the relaxation, and the patient through the therapy being administered.

Effleurage or stroking

Effleurage is performed in a slow, rhythmical, controlled manner using both hands together with a small space between the thumbs. If the therapist wishes to use only light pressure, he or she will use the palms of the hands or the tips of the fingers with light gliding strokes while, for increased pressure, the knuckles or thumbs will be used.

Percussion, drumming or tapotement

Percussion's alternative name tapotement is derived from *tapoter*, a French word that means 'to drum', as of the fingers on a surface. As would be expected from its name, percussion is generally done with the edge of the hand with a quick, chopping movement, although the strokes are not hard. This type of movement would be used on places like the buttocks, thighs, waist or shoulders where there is a wide expanse of flesh.

Friction or pressure

Friction is often used on dancers and athletes who experience problems with damaged ligaments or tendons. This is because the flow of blood is stimulated and the movement of joints is improved. Friction can be performed with the base of the hand, some fingers or the upper part of the thumb. It is not advisable to use this method on parts of the body that have been injured in some way, e.g. where there is bruising.

Petrissage or kneading
Petrissage employs a kneading action on parts of a muscle. As the therapist works across each section, an area of flesh is grasped and squeezed, and this action stimulates the flow of blood and enables tensed muscles to relax. People such as athletes can have an accumulation of lactic acid in certain muscles, and this is why cramp occurs. Parts of the body on which this method is practised are along the stomach and around the waist.

Conclusion
A session may be undertaken in the patient's home, or he or she can attend the masseur or masseuse at a clinic. At each session the client will undress, leaving only pants or briefs on, and will lie on a firm, comfortable surface, such as a table that is designed especially for massage. The massage that follows normally lasts from 20 minutes to one hour. Women in labour have found that the pain experienced during childbirth can be eased if massage is performed on the buttocks and back. The massage eases the buildup of tension in the muscles, encouraging relaxation and easing of

labour pains. It is said to be more effective in women who have previously experienced the benefits and reassurance of massage.

Massage has a wide range of uses for a variety of disorders. Its strengths lie in the easing of strain and tension and inducing relaxation and serenity.

Chiropractic

The word chiropractic originates from two Greek words – *kheir*, which means 'hand', and *praktikos*, which means 'practical'. A school of chiropractic was established in about 1895 by a healer called Daniel Palmer (1845–1913). He was able to cure a man's deafness, which had occurred when he bent down and felt a bone click. Upon examination, Palmer discovered that some bones of the man's spine had become displaced. After successful manipulation the man regained his hearing. Palmer formed the opinion that if there was any displacement in the skeleton this could affect the function of nerves, either increasing or decreasing their action and thereby resulting in a malfunction, i.e. a disease.

Chiropractic is used to relieve pain by manipulation and to correct any problems that are present in joints and muscles but especially in the spine. Like osteopathy, no use is made of surgery or drugs. If there are any spinal disorders they can cause widespread problems elsewhere in the body, such as the hip, leg or arm, and can also initiate lumbago, sciatica, a slipped disc or other back problems. It is even possible that spinal problems can result in seemingly unrelated problems such as catarrh, migraine, asthma, constipation, stress, etc. The majority of a chiropractor's patients, however, suffer mainly from neck and back pain. People suffering from whiplash injuries sustained in car accidents commonly seek the help of a chiropractor. The whiplash effect is caused when the head is violently wrenched either forwards or backwards at the time of impact.

Another common problem that chiropractors treat is headaches, and it is often the case that tension is the underlying cause as it makes the neck muscles contract. Athletes can also obtain relief from injuries such as tennis elbow, pulled muscles, injured ligaments and sprains, etc. As well as the normal methods of manipulating joints, the chiropractor may decide it is necessary to use applications of ice or heat to relieve the injury.

Children can also benefit from treatment by a chiropractor, as there may be some slight accident that occurs in their early years that can reappear in adult life in the form of back pain. It can easily happen, for example, when a child learns to walk and bumps into furniture, or when a baby falls out of a cot. This could result in some damage to the spine that will show only in adult life when a person experiences back pain. At birth, a baby's neck may be injured or the spine may be strained if the use of forceps is necessary, and this can result in headaches and neck problems as he or she grows to maturity. This early type of injury could also account for what is known as 'growing pains', when the real problem is actually damage that has been done to the bones or muscles. To avoid any problems in adult life, chiropractors recommend that children have occasional examinations to detect any damage or displacement in bones and muscles.

As well as babies and children, adults of all ages can benefit from chiropractic. There are some people who regularly take painkillers for painful joints or back pain, but this does not deal with the root cause of the pain, only the symptoms that are produced. It is claimed that chiropractic could be of considerable help in giving treatment to these people. Many pregnant women experience backache at some stage during their pregnancy because of the extra weight that is placed on the spine, and they also may find it difficult keeping their balance. At the time of giving birth, changes take place in the pelvis and joints at the bottom of the spine, and this can be a cause of back pain. Lifting and carrying babies, if not done correctly, can also damage the spine and make the back painful.

It is essential that any chiropractor is fully qualified and registered with the relevant professional association. At the initial visit, a patient will be asked for details of his or her case history, including the present problem, and during the examination painful and tender areas will be noted and joints will be checked to see whether they are functioning correctly or not. X-rays are frequently used by chiropractors since they can show signs of bone disease, fractures or arthritis as well as the spine's condition. After the initial visit, any treatment will normally begin as soon as the patient has been informed of the chiropractor's diagnosis. If it has been decided that chiropractic therapy will not be of any benefit, the patient will be advised accordingly.

For treatment, underwear and/or a robe will be worn, and the patient will either lie, sit or stand on a specially designed couch. Chiropractors use their hands in a skilful way to effect the different manipulative techniques. If it is decided that manipulation is necessary to treat a painful lumbar joint, the patient will need to lie on his or her side. The upper and lower spine will then be rotated manually but in opposite ways. This manipulation will have the effect of partially locking the joint that is being treated, and the upper leg is usually flexed to aid the procedure. The vertebra that is immediately below or above the joint will then be felt by the chiropractor, and the combination of how the patient is lying, coupled with gentle pressure applied by the chiropractor's hand, will move the joint to its farthest extent of normal movement. There will then be a very quick push applied on the vertebra, which results in its movement being extended farther than normal, ensuring that full use of the joint is regained. This is because of the muscles that surround the joint being suddenly stretched, which has the effect of relaxing the muscles of the spine that work upon the joint. This alteration should cause the joint to be able to

be used more naturally and should not be a painful procedure.

There can be a variety of effects felt after treatment – some
patients may feel sore or stiff, or may ache some time after
the treatment, while others will experience the lifting of pain
at once. In some cases there may be a need for multiple
treatments, perhaps four or more, before improvement is
felt. On the whole, problems that have been troubling a patient for a considerable time (chronic) will need more therapy
than anything that occurs quickly and is very painful (acute).

Osteopathy and cranial osteopathy

This is a therapy that aims to pinpoint and treat any problems
that are of a mechanical nature. The body's frame consists
of the skeleton, muscles, joints and ligaments, and all
movements or activities such as running, swimming, eating,
speaking and walking depend upon it. The practice of
osteopathy was originated by Dr Andrew Taylor Still (1828–
1917), an American doctor who came to believe that it would
be safer to encourage the body to heal itself rather than use
the drugs that were then available and that were not always
safe. He regarded the body from an engineer's point of view,
and the combination of this and his medical experience of
anatomy led him to believe that ailments and disorders could
occur when the bones or joints no longer functioned in
harmony. He believed that manipulation was the cure for
the problem. Although his ideas provoked a great deal of

opposition from the American medical profession at first, they slowly came to be accepted. The bulk of scientific research has been done in the United States, with a number of medical schools of osteopathy being established. Dr Martin Littlejohn, who was a pupil of Dr Still, brought the practice of osteopathy to the United Kingdom around 1900, with the first school being founded in 1917 in London.

Problems that prevent the body from working correctly or create pain can be caused by an injury or stress. This can result in what is known as a tension headache since the stress experienced causes a contraction in muscles. These muscles are situated at the back of the neck at the base of the skull, and relief can be obtained by the use of massage. In osteopathy, it is believed that if the basic framework of the body is undamaged, then all physical activities can be accomplished efficiently and without causing any problems. The majority of an osteopath's patients suffer from disorders of the spine, which result in pain in the lower part of the back and the neck. The effects of gravity mean that, even when merely standing, a great deal of constant pressure is exerted on the spinal column and especially on the cartilage between the individual vertebrae. If a person stands incorrectly, with stooped shoulders, this will exacerbate any problems or perhaps initiate one. The joints and framework of the body are manipulated and massaged where necessary so that the usual action is regained.

Athletes or dancers can receive injuries to muscles or joints such as the ankle, hip, wrist or elbow, and they too can benefit from treatment by osteopathy. Pain in the lower back can be experienced by pregnant women, who may stand in a different way as a result of their increasing weight and, if this is the case, osteopathy can often ease matters considerably.

At the first visit to an osteopath, he or she will need to know the complete history of any problems experienced, how they first occurred and what eases or aggravates matters. A patient's case history and any form of therapy that is currently in use will all be of relevance to the practitioner. A thorough examination will then take place, with osteopath observing how the patient sits, stands or lies down and also the manner in which the body is bent to the side, back or front. As each movement takes place, the osteopath is able to take note of the extent and ability of the joint to function. The practitioner will also feel the muscles, soft tissues and ligaments to detect if there is any tension present. Whilst examining the body, the osteopath will note any problems that are present and, as an aid to diagnosis, may also check reflexes, such as the knee-jerk reflex. If a patient has been involved in an accident, X-rays can be checked to determine the extent of any problem. It is possible that a disorder would not benefit from treatment by osteopathy and the patient would be advised accordingly. If this is not the case, treatment can commence with the chosen course of therapy. There is no set number of consultations necessary, as this will depend upon the nature of the problem and also for how long it has been apparent. It is possible that a severe disorder that has arisen suddenly can be alleviated at once.

The osteopath is likely to recommend a number of things so that patients can help themselves between treatments. Techniques such as learning to relax, how to stand and sit correctly and additional exercises may be suggested. Patients generally find that each consultation is quite pleasant and they feel much more relaxed and calm afterwards. The length of each session can vary, but it is generally in the region of half an hour. As the osteopath gently manipulates the joint, it will lessen any tenseness present in the muscles and also improve its ability to work correctly and to its maximum extent. It is this manipulation that can cause a clicking noise to be heard. As well as manipulation, other methods such as massage can be used to good effect. Muscles can be freed from tension if the tissue is massaged and this will also stimulate the flow of blood. In some cases, the patient may experience a temporary deterioration once treatment has commenced, and this is more likely to occur if the ailment has existed for quite some time.

Another form of therapy, which is known as *cranial osteopathy*, can be used for patients suffering from pain in the face or head. This is effected by the osteopath using slight pressure on these areas, including the upper part of the neck. If there is any tautness or tenseness present, the pressure is maintained until the problem improves.

Rolfing

Rolfing is a method of manipulating muscles and connective tissue in order to bring about a correct alignment of the skeleton and other structures. It is based on the premise that many health problems are caused by the development of abnormal alignment, particularly bad posture. The system was devised by Dr Ida Rolf (1896–1979), an American biochemist, who developed it over a long lifetime of helping patients. Once the body's structures are correctly aligned, it is held that gravity and the body's own healing energy will help problems and symptoms to be resolved. Rolfing combines elements of other manipulative techniques and is able to help anyone who feels that there is a misalignment or who has difficulties relating to posture.

Iridology

Iridology is a diagnostic technique often used in naturopathy. It is held that the iris (the coloured part of the eye, which is a muscular disc that controls the diameter of the pupil and hence the amount of light allowed to enter) reveals clues about the health of the body. Each part of the body is held to have its corresponding point in an iris and patterns of fibres, marks or spots are believed to indicate the health of the area involved. In addition, ten fibre patterns are recognised, which point to a particular type of constitution. Iridology is a gentle and non-stressful method of examination, somewhat similar to an eye test, in which the therapist takes detailed photographs of the eyes for further reference. The results, along with other findings, can help a naturopath to decide upon a helpful course of treatment or other appropriate recommendations.

Hydrotherapy

Hydrotherapy is the use of water to heal and ease a variety of ailments, and the water may be used in a number of different ways. The healing properties of water have been recognised since ancient times, notably by the Greek, Roman and Turkish civilisations but also by people in Europe and China. Most people know the benefits of a hot bath in relaxing the body, relieving muscular aches and stiffness, and helping to bring about restful sleep. Hot water or steam causes blood vessels to dilate, opens skin pores and stimulates perspiration, and relaxes limbs and muscles. A cold bath or shower acts in the opposite way and is refreshing and invigorating. The cold causes blood vessels in the skin to constrict and blood is diverted to internal tissues and organs to maintain the core temperature of the body. Applications of cold water or ice reduce swelling and bruising and cause skin pores to close.

Treatment techniques in hydrotherapy

Hot baths
Hot baths are used to ease muscle and joint pains and inflammation. Warm or hot baths, with the addition of various substances such as seaweed extract to the water,

may also be used to help the healing of some skin conditions or minor wounds. After childbirth, frequent bathing in warm water to which an appropriate herbal preparation may be added is recommended to heal skin tears.

Cold baths

Cold baths are used to improve blood flow to internal tissues and organs and to reduce swellings. The person may sit for a moment in shallow cold water with additional water being splashed onto exposed skin. An inflamed, painful part may be immersed in cold water to reduce swelling. The person is not allowed to become chilled, and this form of treatment is best suited for those able to dry themselves rapidly with a warm towel. It is not advisable for people with serious conditions or for the elderly or very young.

Steam baths

Steam baths, along with saunas and Turkish baths, are used to encourage sweating and the opening of skin pores, and they have a cleansing and refreshing effect. The body may be able to eliminate harmful substances in this way and treatment finishes with a cool bath.

Sitz baths

Sitz baths are usually given as a treatment for painful conditions with broken skin, such as piles or anal fissure, and also for ailments affecting the urinary and genital organs.

The person sits in a specially designed bath that has two compartments, one with warm water, the other with cold. First, the person sits in the warm water, which covers the lower abdomen and hips, with the feet in the cold water compartment. After three minutes, the patient changes round and sits in the cold water with the feet in the warm compartment. The name comes from the German *Sitzbad*, 'seat bath'.

Hot and cold sprays
Hot and cold sprays of water may be given for a number of different disorders but are not recommended for those with serious illnesses, elderly people or young children.

Wrapping
Wrapping is used for feverish conditions, backache and bronchitis. A cold wet sheet that has been squeezed out is wrapped around the person, followed by a dry sheet and warm blanket. These are left in place until the inner sheet has dried and the coverings are then removed. The body is sponged with tepid water (at blood heat) before being dried with a towel. Sometimes the wrap is applied to a smaller area of the body, such as the lower abdomen, to ease a particular problem, usually constipation.

In orthodox medicine, hydrotherapy is used as a technique of physiotherapy for people recovering from serious injuries with problems of muscle wastage. Also, it is used for people with joint problems and those with severe physical disabilities. Many hospitals also offer the choice of a water birth to expectant mothers, and this has become an increasingly popular method of childbirth. Hydrotherapy may be offered as a form of treatment for other medical conditions in naturopathy, using the techniques listed above. It is wise to obtain medical advice before proceeding with hydrotherapy, and this is especially important for elderly persons, children and those with serious conditions or illnesses.

Examples of Naturopathic Treatment for Particular Disorders

Acne vulgaris

Acne vulgaris is a disorder of the skin that most commonly occurs in both sexes at puberty, but particularly in boys. It is characterised by the presence of pustules (whiteheads and blackheads), which usually occur on the face, neck, chest, shoulders and upper back. Sebaceous glands in the skin become overactive as a result of a surge in androgens (male hormones) such as testosterone. There is a greater production of sebum (the oily secretion of the glands) which favours a proliferation of skin bacteria and consequent infection. The hair follicles become blocked, and if this is complete, whiteheads form or, if incomplete, blackheads. In addition, research has shown that about half of acne sufferers have increased levels of toxins in their blood which may be caused by exposure to environmental chemicals, including cosmetic preparations, industrial pollutants and drugs. Also, there is now evidence to suggest that glucose tolerance in the skin of some acne sufferers is impaired, with increased insulin insensitivity.

Diet

Sugar, refined carbohydrates, fried foods, milk and dairy products should be excluded. A wholefood diet high in fibre should be eaten. A high fibre diet reduces the likelihood of toxins being absorbed.

Vitamins and minerals

Vitamin A – inhibits production of sebum.

Vitamin B complex – involved in hormone metabolism; deficiency may increase sensitivity to testosterone.

Vitamin C – antioxidant activity.

Vitamin E – regulates vitamin A and, with selenium, has important free radical activity.

Selenium – important free radical activity.

Chromium (Brewer's yeast) – increases insulin sensitivity in the skin. Insulin is known to improve acne.

Herbal medicines

Echinacea augustifolia (purple coneflower) – antibacterial activity, enhances the immune system, promotes the healing of wounds and reduces inflammation.

Hydrastis canadensis (goldenseal) – antibacterial activity, promotes liver detoxification and kills off harmful bowel bacteria that produce toxins.

Taraxacum officinale (dandelion) – supports the liver and promotes bile flow.

Silybum marianum (milk thistle) – supports and protects the liver through its content of silymarin, which is a potent antioxidant. Hence promotes detoxification.

Lifestyle factors

Self-confidence is frequently low in a person with acne as the condition can be unsightly and a cause of depression. Exercise and restful sleep are important in increasing the sense of wellbeing. All cosmetic preparations should be avoided but the skin can be cleansed with a sulphur or calendula-containing soap. Other natural herbal preparations that can be used as healing and antibacterial washes include comfrey, calendula, camomile, lavender, yarrow and elder.

Asthma

Asthma is a common condition characterised by breathing difficulties caused by narrowing of the airways (bronchi) of the lung. Asthma is a hypersensitive condition that can be brought on by exposure to a variety of allergens (allergy-provoking substances), exertion, stress or infections. An asthma sufferer may have other hypersensitive conditions such as eczema and hay fever. The characteristic symptoms are wheezing and shortness of breath, which, in a severe attack, can cause death.

Diet

Food allergy is a contributory or causative, factor in some cases of asthma. Suspect foods include eggs, peanuts, shellfish, nuts, wheat products, chocolate, milk, food additives and colourings, and citrus fruits. Wholefoods should be eaten and a vegan diet has proved to be beneficial. Onions and garlic are helpful as they appear to help to inhibit the inflammatory process.

Vitamins and minerals

Vitamin B_{12} – patients with asthma provoked by food allergy sometimes produce low levels of stomach acid which is linked with B_{12} deficiency. Supplements of this vitamin help to redress the balance and improve asthma.

Vitamin B_6 – may be deficient in its most active form in the blood of asthmatics. Supplementation appears to improve asthma indirectly in some people, although the mechanism behind this is not clear.

Vitamin C – ascorbic acid levels are often low in the blood of asthmatics. Vitamin C may reduce bronchial constriction and has important antioxidant activity.

Vitamin E and selenium – antioxidant and anti-inflammatory activity through inhibition of the production of leukotrienes. These substances are naturally produced by white blood cells and are probably involved in the allergic response.

Magnesium – may relax smooth muscle and hence help to prevent bronchial constriction.

Herbal medicines

Ephedra sineca – contains ephedrine and other compounds which have anti-allergic and anti-inflammatory activity.

Scutellaria baicalensis (Chinese skullcap) – anti-allergic and anti-inflammatory. Contains flavonoids, which have potent antioxidant activity and are able to inactivate free radicals.

Lobelia inflata (Indian tobacco) – helps relaxation of bronchial muscle; expectorant activity. The active ingredient is an alkaloid substance called lobeline.

Glycyrrhiza glabra (liquorice root) – anti-allergic, anti-inflammatory.

Angelica sinensis (angelica) – anti-allergic activity.

Capsicum frutescens (Chilli pepper) – contains capsaicin, which helps to protect the lining of the airways against substances that may provoke an irritant response.

Thea sinensis (green tea) – contains theophylline, which acts as a bronchodilator through relaxation of smooth muscle. Antioxidant activity.

Symphlocarpus factida (skunk cabbage) – respiratory sedative and expectorant. Usually used with chilli pepper and Indian tobacco to calm an acute attack.

Lifestyle factors

Management of stress, relaxation and breathing exercises are very important in the management of asthma. Massage and hydrotherapy may also be recommended.

Atherosclerosis

Atherosclerosis is a degenerative disease of the arteries in which there is a buildup of fatty deposits on the inner walls. This causes a reduction in blood flow and an increased likelihood of such conditions as hypertension, angina, stroke and heart attack. It is associated with the Western lifestyle of obesity, lack of exercise, smoking and eating a diet high in animal fat.

Diet

A wholefood diet should be eaten that is high in fibre, low in fats and in which starches and complex carbohydrates are the main components. The fats eaten should be in the form of vegetable oils and not derived from animal sources or dairy products. The latter foods should be eaten only occasionally and low fat varieties chosen. Oily fish should be eaten two or three times a week. Plenty of onions and garlic should be included as these may help to lower blood cholesterol, prevent the clumping together of platelets and promote beneficial HDLs (high density lipoproteins). Lecithin from plant sources such as soya beans, ginger and alfalfa leaves are similarly beneficial.

Vitamins and minerals

Vitamin B_6 – involved in preventing the factors which encourage the development of atherosclerosis, including the clumping together of platelets (structures involved in blood clotting).

Vitamin C – deficiency can lead to elevated levels of blood cholesterol. Maintains the health of arterial walls and is involved in metabolic regulation of fats.

Vitamin E – inactivates free radicals, which damage arterial walls; promotes HDLs (high density lipoproteins), which protect against atherosclerosis by removing cholesterol; reduces the clumping together of platelets.

Magnesium – promotes the health of arteries; increases the levels of beneficial HDLs (high-density lipoproteins); reduces the clumping together of platelets.

Carnitine – a naturally occurring compound with some similarities to vitamins, which is found in heart and other muscle and some tissues. It is manufactured within the body by the liver, kidneys and brain and is involved in the transport of fatty acids within cells. Deficiency is found in several forms of heart disease, and it is beneficial in the treatment of these and of atherosclerosis.

Lifestyle factors
For both prevention and treatment, it is essential to give up smoking and to take up a regular form of exercise. Consumption of coffee and alcohol should be reduced to a low level.

Depression
Depression is a mental state of extreme sadness and pessi-

mism in which normal behaviour patterns are disturbed. It is accompanied by feelings of worthlessness and guilt, tiredness, lack of interest and pleasure in activities and people, loss of concentration and the ability to think clearly, and thoughts of death and suicide. There is often sleep disturbance, appetite and weight loss or, alternatively, overeating and weight gain and lack of physical and social activities and interactions. Most people experience feelings of depression at some stage in life, often related to traumatic events such as bereavement or loss of employment. However, the state must be present for at least one month for a person to be termed clinically depressed. Depression may have an organic element, such as disruption of certain biochemical factors within the brain, possibly caused by a nutrient deficiency. Naturopathic treatment can help to support conventional therapy.

Diet
A wholefood diet should be eaten, and foods commonly associated with allergy (e.g. eggs, peanuts, shellfish, nuts, wheat products, chocolate, milk, cheese, food additives and colourings, citrus fruits) should be avoided. Caffeine (in coffee and tea) should be excluded.

Vitamins and minerals
Deficiency of any of these can contribute to depression:
Vitamin B complex

Vitamin B$_{12}$
Folic acid
Magnesium
Other supplements – amino acids, possibly.

Herbal medicines
St John's wort; herbal teas, particularly borage, vervain or rosemary.

Lifestyle factors
A regular exercise programme is excellent in the treatment of depression and helps to restore normal appetite and sleeping patterns. Relaxation exercises, visualization therapy, colour and dance movement therapy and hypnotherapy can all be of benefit in individual cases.

Other therapies
Massage, aromatherapy and acupuncture may all be beneficial as can hydrotherapy, especially sauna baths.

Eczema

Eczema is an inflammatory condition of the skin that causes itching, a red rash and, often, the formation of small blisters that weep and become encrusted. This may be followed by the skin thickening and then peeling off in scales. There are several types of eczema, with the form known as atopic being one of the most common. This is the hereditary tendency to form an immediate allergy reaction as a result of the presence of an antibody in the skin. Eczema is often accompanied by asthma and hay fever.

Diet
Food allergy can be a cause of eczema, and a diet eliminating the common allergic foods may be recommended, at least until symptoms improve. Eating a raw fruit/vegetable diet for a short period may be particularly beneficial. Oily fish containing EPA (eicosapentaenoic acid) should be eaten two or three times a week as this is of proven benefit in improving the condition.

Vitamins and minerals
Vitamin A – essential for health of the skin; deficiency may be a cause of thickening in eczema.
Vitamin C
Vitamin E
Zinc
Other nutrients
Bioflavonoids – coloured compounds present in fruits and berries which have anti-inflammatory and anti-allergy properties.
Evening primrose oil
Flaxseed oil

Herbal medicines
Prunus spinosa (blackthorn) berry
Crataegus monogyna (hawthorn) berry
Vaccinium myrtillus (bilberry) leaf
Arctium lappa (burdock) root
Ointment or topical solutions:
Glycyrrhiza glabra (liquorice root)
Calendula officinalis (marigold)
Matricaria chamomilla (Germal chamomile)

Lifestyle factors
Avoidance of all chemicals and harsh detergents is essential and also irritant fibres such as wool. A mild herbal soap, e.g. containing chamomile, may be used. Measures to avoid stress are important since eczema is made worse by stressful situations.

Gallstones

Gallstones are deposits of varying composition that form in the gall bladder, apparently as a result of a change in the composition of bile which renders cholesterol or some other substance less soluble. This then precipitates to form a stone, or one may begin to develop around a foreign body. Stones are of three main types: cholesterol, pigment and mixed, the latter being most common. Calcium salts are usually found in varying amounts and are the most common mineral present. Gallstones may be present for years without producing symptoms, but can cause severe pain and may pass into the common bile duct, where the obstruction results in jaundice.

Diet
A high fibre, wholefood diet should be eaten, with minimal consumption of animal fats and dairy produce. The mucilaginous fibres contained in fruits and vegetables, oats, etc, are particularly useful for their effect upon cholesterol. Gallstones are less common in vegetarians. Fried foods should be avoided. At least six glasses of water should be drunk each day so that this is available for bile secretion.

Vitamins and minerals, other nutritional factors
Vitamin C
Vitamin E
The following promote factors relating to fat metabolism and the lowering of cholesterol:
Vitamin B_{12}
Choline
L-methionine

Herbal medicines
The following all act as choleretics promoting bile production:
Taraxacum officinale (dandelion root)
Silybum marianum (silymarin)
Curcuma longa (turmeric)

Cynara scolymus (artichoke leaves)
Peumus boldo (boldo)

A combination of terpenes (aromatic hydrocarbons) derived from plants has been used to dissolve gallstones and can be a successful form of treatment. The combination includes such substances as menthol and has proved to be a safe form of treatment but one that must be prescribed by a doctor.

Haemorrhoids

Haemorrhoids, or piles, are varicose and inflamed veins around the lower end of the bowel, situated in the wall of the anus. They are classified as internal, external and mixed, depending upon whether they appear beyond the anus. They are commonly caused by constipation or diarrhoea, especially in middle and older age, and may be exacerbated by a sedentary lifestyle. They may also occur as a result of childbearing. Symptoms of haemorrhoids are bleeding, which appears bright red, and discomfort, itching and pain which may be acute.

Diet

Diet is considered by all health practitioners to be the major factor in the development, or otherwise, of haemorrhoids. They are practically unknown among peoples who habitually eat unrefined foods with a high fibre content. Haemorrhoids are very much related to the unhealthy Western lifestyle and hence, in both prevention and treatment, adoption of a wholefood, high fibre diet is of prime importance. Plenty of fruits, particularly berries (blackberries, bilberries, cherries, blackcurrants), vegetables and mucilaginous fibre should be eaten, which help to produce softer, bulkier stools that are easier to pass. (Smaller, drier, harder stools that result from a low fibre diet, are difficult to pass and produce constipation and straining – all factors that favour the development of haemorrhoids.) The soluble fibres are generally more useful than wheat bran, which can be irritant.

Vitamins, minerals and nutritional supplements
Vitamin A
Vitamin B
Vitamin C
Vitamin E
Zinc
Flavonoids – strengthen veins

Herbal medicines
Ruscus aculeatus (butcher's broom) – strengthens the walls of veins.

Topical preparations
Solutions or ointments containing *Symphytum officinale* (comfrey), *Hamamelis virginiana* (witch hazel), *Myroxylon pereirae* (Peruvian balsam), *Aesculus hippocastanum* (horse chestnut), cocoa butter or cod liver oil can provide soothing relief.

Hydrotherapy

A sitz bath using warm water is a soothing and cleansing treatment for haemorrhoids.

Lifestyle changes

A factor in the development of haemorrhoids is a sedentary lifestyle. For both prevention and treatment, regular exercise, which stimulates the circulation and promotes bowel regularity, is important.

Hypertension

Hypertension is high arterial blood pressure, which may be classified as either essential or malignant. Essential hypertension may be of unknown cause or result from diseases of the kidneys or endocrine system. Malignant hypertension is fatal, if not treated, and may be an end stage of the essential form or a condition in itself. It tends to occur in younger age groups and is often accompanied by kidney failure. Atherosclerosis is a complication of, and often associated with, hypertension. Other complications include cerebral haemorrhage and heart and kidney failure. Hypertension carries an increased risk of death or incapacity through strokes, heart and cardiovascular diseases. It is strongly associated with the unhealthy Western lifestyle, particularly a diet high in fat, salt and sugar and low in fibre, obesity, lack of exercise and stress.

Diet

Obesity is a major contributory factor in the development

of hypertension. Adopting a wholefood diet that is high in fibre and complex carbohydrates and low in fat and from which sugar is eliminated should lead to a gradual weight loss. If necessary, a weight-reduction diet may be recommended. The foods chosen should include those that are high in potassium and low in sodium. No salt should be added to meals at any stage. It should be remembered that manufactured foods are often high in salt and so these should be eaten as little as possible and low-salt varieties chosen.

Sugar also raises blood pressure, and amounts eaten should be reduced. Foods containing calcium, magnesium and linolenic acid should be eaten as these substances have a hypotensive effect. Garlic and onions are useful and should be eaten freely as these also can help to lower blood pressure. Berries containing flavonoids are beneficial. Coffee and alcohol consumption should be reduced.

Vitamins and minerals

Vitamin C – promotes health of blood vessels

Calcium and magnesium – hypotensive activity

Zinc – lead and cadmium levels may be high in people with hypertension. Zinc is helpful in counteracting the effects of cadmium hypertension.

Herbal medicines

Crataegus monogyna (hawthorn) – extracts of the berries, leaves and flowers have hypotensive activity and also reduce the level of blood cholesterol.

Viscum album (mistletoe) – acts as an anti-hypertensive; must be used only as directed by a naturopathic doctor.

Lifestyle factors

Smoking is a major factor in the development of hypertension and must be given up. Regular exercise is important in preventing the development of hypertension but should only be undertaken under medical advice for those who have the condition. Measures to control stress are also vital, both in prevention and treatment.

Irritable bowel syndrome (IBS)

Irritable bowel syndrome is a condition caused by abnormal muscular contractions (or increased motility) in the colon, producing effects in the large and small intestines. Symptoms include pain in the abdomen which changes location, disturbed bowel movements with intermittent bouts of diarrhoea and constipation, heartburn and feelings of bloatedness. The cause is now known but a number of contributory factors may be involved, including diet, food sensitivity or intolerance and anxiety and stress.

Diet

A naturopath may suspect that food intolerance is responsible for the symptoms of IBS and may recommend a hypoallergenic (low allergy) diet of simple foods. Usually, a person is placed on this elimination or restricted diet for up to one month to see if this brings about an improvement in symptoms. If symptoms improve, usual foods are gradually reintroduced and the reactions noted. Coffee, spices and alcohol should be eliminated from the diet because of their irritant effects.

Increasing the amount of fibre in the diet is another method of treatment which can bring about a relief of symptoms. In general, wheat bran is not recommended because of its known connection with food allergy. The most useful forms of fibre are the water-soluble types as found in oats, fruit and vegetables and peas and beans. Psyllium seed and linseed oil are useful, natural laxatives.

Herbal remedies

Peppermint oil – enteric-coated capsules are recommended which are resistant to stomach acid and dissolve in the bowel. Peppermint oil calms and reduces muscle activity and relieves abdominal symptoms.

The following all have calming and damping down qualities:

Matricaria chamomilla (chamomile)

Melissa officinalis (balm)

Rosmarinus officinalis (rosemary)

Zingiber officinale (ginger)

Valeriana officinalis (valerian)

Lifestyle factors

Counselling, ways of managing stress, including regular exercise and relaxation techniques are vital components in bringing about an improvement in IBS.

Other therapies, including massage, hydrotherapy and aromatherapy, may provide soothing relief.

Kidney stones

Kidney stones are small deposits of 'gravel', consisting mainly of calcium salts and smaller amounts of uric acid, which crystallise out from urine. If they form in the kidneys, they do not usually produce symptoms but if they pass into the ureters (the tubes that connect with the bladder), they may cause blockage and severe pain (renal colic). There is also an increased likelihood of urinary infection. A number of diseases and conditions increase the risk of kidney stones. Kidney stones that are producing symptoms must be treated by conventional medicine in the first instance. The naturopathic approach is valuable in prevention and in decreasing the likelihood of recurrence, particularly by adjustments to the diet.

Diet

A number of aspects of the Western diet increase the risk and incidence of kidney stones. These include eating low fibre, highly refined carbohydrates and too much animal fat and protein. A high intake of salt, vitamin D and calcium in foods are further contributory factors along with over-consumption of alcohol. A naturopathic wholefood diet, rich in fibre and complex carbohydrates, vegetables and fruits and low in animal fats and proteins, helps to prevent kidney stones. A person who has had the condition will almost certainly need to limit their intake of calcium in foods (milk, cheese, dairy produce) and also oxalic acid (rhubarb, parsley, beet, spinach, cranberries, chocolate). (Increased calcium intake, especially for women, is advocated to decrease the risk of osteoporosis. Supplements, in the form of calcium citrate, do not increase the risk of kidney stones.) Plenty of water should be drunk to help flush out the kidneys and make the urine more dilute.

Vitamins and minerals

Magnesium citrate and Vitamin B6 – may be deficient. The magnesium should be in the form of citrate, which inhibits stone formation.

Vitamin K – necessary for the production of a glycoprotein which inhibits the growth of calcium stones.

Herbal remedies

Ammi visnaga (khella) – an ancient Egyptian remedy facilitating relaxation of the ureters so that a stone may pass more easily.

The following contain organic compounds called anthraquinones which inhibit the formation of calcium stones:

Aloe vera

Cassia fistula (cassia pods)

Rubia tinctoria (madder root)

Osteoarthritis

Osteoarthritis is a form of arthritis involving degeneration of the joint cartilage with accompanying changes in the associated bone. It usually involves the loss of cartilage and the development of osteophytes (abnormal bony projections) at the bone margins. The function of the joint (most commonly the thumb, knee and hip) is affected and it becomes painful. The condition may be caused by overuse or general wear and tear and commonly affects those past middle age. It may also result from trauma or some other joint disorder. Early symptoms include stiffness upon arising in the morning or following rest. Later there is pain with movement, which is eased by rest. Conventional treatment involves drug therapy and replacement surgery.

Diet

A wholefood diet based on unrefined, complex carbohydrates and plenty of fibre should be eaten, with low consumption of animal fats. The correct weight should be maintained to avoid placing stress on joints. In some people, alkaloids found in plants of the *Solanaceae* family (tomatoes, egg plant, potatoes, peppers – and also tobacco and deadly nightshade) may contribute to osteoarthritis, and these vegetables should not be eaten. Berries rich in flavonoids should be eaten freely.

Vitamins and minerals

Vitamin C – essential for health of connective tissue and cartilage

Vitamin E – antioxidant properties. (Combinations of C and E appear to have enhanced beneficial effects.)

Pantothenic acid (vitamin B_5)

Vitamin B_6

Vitamin A

Zinc

Copper

Herbal remedies

Yucca – endotoxins produced by gut bacteria and absorbed into the body reduce the efficiency of cartilage repair. A substance, saponin, contained in yucca may reduce endotoxin absorption, hence promoting the repair of cartilage. Other herbs may have a similar effect.

Harpagophytum procumbens (Devil's claw) – contains potent glycosides and may have anti-inflammatory and analgesic effects.

Other therapies

Specific isometric exercises may be recommended, and other activities, especially swimming, are beneficial. Hydrotherapy, possibly including salt-water bathing, may help some sufferers. The use of heat and cold (ice) and diathermy (electric current – short wave) can be beneficial. Physical therapies such as massage and osteopathy must be used very cautiously. Acupuncture can bring significant relief for some sufferers with osteoarthritis. Aromatherapy with gentle massage, using chamomile, rosemary, lavender and marigold oils, may be helpful. Relaxation techniques are beneficial, as are measures to combat stress, which may exacerbate arthritis.

Osteoporosis

Osteoporosis is a loss of bone tissue so that the bones become thin and brittle and susceptible to fractures. It is not only calcium and other minerals that are lost but also the protein and collagen components that form the matrix. The condition is common in postmenopausal women and is related to a decline in the hormone oestrogen, which is protective before the menopause. However, it can also result from long-term use of steroid drugs. Osteoporosis can also affect men, although it is usually less severe because of greater bone density in most males. The conventional approach for women is hormone replacement therapy and calcium supplements.

Diet
Osteoporosis is commonly believed to be related to a calcium deficiency that can be simply overcome by increasing dietary intake. However, of greater significance are the metabolic factors that affect calcium utilisation and availability within the body, and these can be directly affected by diet. For example, a diet high in protein, phosphates and refined sugar, common in Western countries, increases the

amount of calcium eliminated from the body in urine. Also, some people with osteoporosis have low levels of acid in their stomach and are less able to absorb calcium effectively. Coffee and alcohol may also contribute to elimination of calcium from the body. In general, for both prevention and treatment, a diet rich in vegetables and fruits, seeds, nuts and cereals and low in animal protein and fat should be eaten. Berries rich in flavonoids, e.g. blackberries, should be eaten freely as they help maintain the structural protein components (collagen) of bone. Carbonated drinks, coffee and alcohol should be eliminated or drunk only sparingly.

Vitamins and minerals

Vitamin B_6, Vitamin B_{12}, folic acid – all important in enzyme activity and, if deficient, lead to a rise in blood levels of homocysteine, a compound that may be involved in the development of osteoporosis.

Vitamin K – important for maintaining the protein components of bone.

Calcium citrate – the most readily utilised form of calcium, which does not increase the risk of kidney stones.

Magnesium citrate – magnesium is involved in vitamin D activity which, in turn, is vital in calcium metabolism. It is often deficient in people with osteoporosis who may then, also, be lacking in the most potent form of vitamin D. Vitamin D itself may not be deficient and supplements should only be taken cautiously.

Boron – necessary for vitamin D and hormone activity, specifically for conversion of the vitamin into its most potent form in the kidneys.

Strontium – naturally found in bones and confers strength.

Herbal medicines

Plants with oestrogenic activity, i.e. which contain substances called phytoestrogens that act in a similar way to the hormone oestrogen, may help in the prevention and treatment of menopausal osteoporosis. Phytoestrogens are generally less potent than both naturally occurring and synthetic oestrogen and do not produce unwarranted side effects. Those that may be used include:

Cimicifuga racemosa (black cohosh)

Helonias opulus (false unicorn root)

Glycyrrhiza glabra (liquorice)

Aletris farinosa (unicorn root)

Foeniculum vulgare (fennel)

Angelica sinensis (dong quai)

Lifestyle factors

Exercise is vital for maintaining the strength of bones and ensuring that they have a good supply of calcium. Weight-bearing exercises are particularly beneficial, with walking being one of the best forms, particularly for older people. As with so many illnesses, smoking increases the risk of developing osteoporosis and is one of the factors that may contribute towards the elimination of calcium from the body. A person with existing osteoporosis has to be careful to avoid falls and accidents that might cause fractures, but gentle exercise is beneficial. Hip fractures are particularly common in osteoporosis.

Prostate gland enlargement

Prostate gland enlargement (benign prostatic hypertrophy or BPH) is an enlargement of the prostate gland that commonly occurs in older men. The condition causes pressure to be exerted on the neck of the bladder, obstructing the flow of urine. The bladder consequently extends, and there is a frequent need to pass urine, especially during the night, discomfort, pain and 'dribbling'. Since the bladder is not being emptied effectively, infection is common, which may, in severe cases, involve the upper urinary tract and kidneys. A man with symptoms of BPH should always have medical investigations to rule out the possibility of malignancy. Conventional treatment is to remove surgically the prostate gland (prostatectomy). Naturopaths believe that measures can be taken both to relieve and prevent prostate problems, and these may be worth considering, even by men who are awaiting surgery.

Diet
There is a suspicion among naturopaths that the increasingly

common incidence of BPH in the modern world may be related to the high levels of pollutants such as heavy metals and pesticides in the environment. Eating a wholefood diet that is rich in fibre, vitamins, minerals, flavonoids and carotenes aids the body's natural detoxification processes and lowers blood cholesterol levels. (Accumulation of cholesterol and its metabolic products in prostate gland cells is a factor in both BPH and malignancy.) Oily fish and vegetable oils should be included. Alcohol consumption should be minimal.

Vitamins, minerals and nutritional supplements
Zinc as picolinate or citrate, Vitamin B_6 – involved in hormone and enzyme metabolism; limit the accumulation of forms of testosterone (male hormones) in the prostate gland, which occurs in BPH. The end result is a reduction in the size of the prostate gland.
Essential fatty acids from evening primrose, sunflower, linseed, walnut or soya oil – can improve symptoms in some patients.
Amino acids (glutamic acid, glycine, alanine) – may relieve symptoms in some patients.

Herbal remedies
Serenoa repens (saw palmetto berries) – extract appears to improve BPH by inhibiting the processes affecting dihydrotestosterone (a form of the male hormone, testosterone) within the prostate gland. Diuretic.

Panax ginseng (Chinese/Korean ginseng)
Flower pollen
Agropyron repens (couch grass) – diuretic
Equisetum arvense (horsetail) – diuretic

Lifestyle factors
Smoking and drinking alcohol have adverse effects and consumption of tea and coffee should also be limited. Regular exercise is beneficial.

Other therapies
Hydrotherapy, particularly in the form of sitz baths, is a recommended naturopathic treatment for BPH. Hot sitz baths are most commonly used in initial treatment, as long as there is no inflammation or infection present.

Psoriasis

Psoriasis is a chronic skin disease, the exact cause of which is unknown but in which there is an accelerated rate of cell division, leading to the appearance of thickened, red patches. The affected skin appears as scaly, red areas that may itch, usually starting around the elbows, knees, wrists, ankles or scalp. In half the cases, there is a family history of the condition, and it can be made worse by stress and anxiety. In conventional medicine, treatment involves the use of ointments, creams, drugs, vitamin A and ultraviolet light. In some people, a form of arthritis can occur, associated with the condition.

Diet

A number of digestive factors may contribute towards the development of psoriasis, including poor digestion of protein and absorption of toxins produced by gut bacteria. A high fibre diet containing plenty of fruit and vegetables is essential for binding bacterial endotoxins and promoting their elimination in faeces. Pineapple and papaya fruit contain useful protein-digesting enzymes and should be included in the diet. Some naturopaths may recommend supplementation with an extract of proteolytic enzymes. Oily fish should be eaten every day or a supplement of oils (eicosapentaenoic acid – EPA) taken. EPA inhibits the formation of leukotrienes (inflammatory compounds) derived from arachidonic acids found in animal tissues. Leukotrienes are present at a very high level in the skin of people with psoriasis, and it is beneficial to keep the consumption of all foods of animal origin at a low level. Alcohol may be a causal factor in psoriasis in some individuals and so intake should be limited to a low level.

Vitamins, minerals and nutritional supplements

Vitamin A – essential for skin health

Vitamin E and selenium – antioxidant activity

Folic acid

Zinc – normalises copper/zinc balance in blood; may be deficient in people with psoriasis; has anti-inflammatory activity.

Eicosapentaenoic acid (EPA)

Herbal remedies

Smilax aristolochiaefolia (South American sarsaparilla or bamboo briar) – extract is able to bind bacterial endotoxins.

Silybum marianum (milk thistle) – contains silymarin, a flavonoid which supports the liver and reduces inflammation.

Momardica charantia (bitter melon, balsam pear) – inhibits an enzyme involved in skin cell proliferation.

Ointments or creams containing comfrey or chamomile are soothing and help to relieve itching.

Other therapies

Detoxification by fasting – psoriasis has been shown to improve with controlled fasting in some studies, probably because of the removal of harmful bacterial endotoxins.

Varicose veins

Varicose veins are veins that have become stretched, distended and twisted. The superficial veins in the legs are the ones that are most commonly involved, and symptoms include pain or a dragging, heavy sensation. More rarely, ulceration may occur, and varicose veins are common in middle-aged and elderly people, particularly women. The condition is usually not serious but is uncomfortable and unsightly. Causes include congenital, defective valves in the veins, obesity, pregnancy and thrombophlebitis. Treatment in conventional medicine involves the wearing of elasticated support stockings, sclerotherapy (injection of various solutions) and phlebectomy (surgical removal of affected veins).

Diet

Weight reduction may be advised if a person is obese. The most common factor in varicose veins is a lack of dietary fibre, and the condition can be prevented or improved when intake is increased. The most useful forms are the mucilaginous fibres contained in fruits, vegetables, oats, etc. The diet should contain plenty of flavonoid-rich berries (blackberries, bilberries, cherries, blackcurrants, etc), which strengthen the vein walls and enhance circulation. Garlic, onions, ginger and cayenne help to reduce the formation of fibrin (a product of blood clotting) and improve blood flow through the veins, so reducing pressure. Pineapple also contains a protein-digesting enzyme that has a similar beneficial effect. All these substances should be eaten freely.

Vitamins, minerals and nutritional supplements
Vitamin C
Vitamin E
Zinc

Herbal medicines
Centella asiatica (gotu kola) – strengthens connective tissue and enhances circulation.

Aesculus hippocastanum (horse chestnut) – strengthens vein walls.

Ruscus aculeatus (butcher's broom) – contains compounds known as niscogenins which have beneficial effects on veins and anti-inflammatory activity.

Vaccinum myrtillus (bilberry) – extract of berries to strengthen veins.

Lifestyle factors

Exercise is extremely important in preventing and treating varicose veins by enhancing the circulation of blood as muscles are contracting. Exercise such as walking, cycling, dancing, etc, is of particular benefit as the leg muscles are actively used. It is important to avoid standing for extended periods as this is known to encourage the development of varicose veins. Resting with the legs raised up and avoiding sitting with crossed legs are further beneficial measures. Wearing elasticated supports on the legs is helpful.

Other therapies

Hydrotherapy and exercises for the legs are measures that may be recommended.

Good Health in Older Age

Adopting a holistic, naturopathic lifestyle promotes good health at all stages in life. In older age, however, the benefits are particularly important and may even help to slow down the natural processes of ageing. As they approach older age, many people become deficient in essential nutritional elements, sometimes because these are less efficiently absorbed by the digestive system. This in turn can lead to the appearance of diseases and disorders. In addition, there is now some evidence to suggest that the cumulative effects of attack by free radicals within the body contribute significantly both to ageing and certain diseases, including some cancers, which are more likely to appear in older age. For many people, advancing age brings an increase in the number of stressful life events which may be, to a large extent, unavoidable.

In all these aspects, a naturopathic lifestyle helps to restore a natural balance, strengthening a person both physically and mentally and promoting wellbeing in this important period.

Diet

A varied wholefood diet, rich in vitamins, minerals and natural antioxidants, should be eaten. (The digestive system can become more sensitive in older age, and foods that are known to cause upset should be avoided.) It is important to keep a check on weight and adjust overall intake if necessary. However, a person following a naturopathic diet is far less likely to gain weight. Fresh vegetables and fruit should be eaten freely, although specific recommendations may be made if a particular disease or condition exists. There is a natural tendency for the arteries to harden (atherosclerosis) with advancing age, but following a naturopathic diet has been proved to be protective.

Vitamins, minerals and nutritional supplements

A general multi-vitamin/mineral supplement designed for older people may be recommended.

Vitamin C, Vitamin E, Selenium – antioxidants; boost immune system

The following boost natural antioxidant enzymes in body, e.g. glutathione peroxidase, catalase and superoxide dismutase

Vitamin E

Selenium

Beta-carotene or carotenes

flavonoids

sulphur-containing amino acids (methionine and cysteine)

Herbal remedies

Several may be beneficial, particularly those that have natural antioxidant and anti-free radical activity. These include:

Silybum marianum (milk thistle) – flavonoids that support
the liver.

Ginkgo biloba (ginkgo tree) – flavonoids that support the
thyroid and adrenal glands and promote the supply of
blood to the brain.

Panax ginseng (ginseng)

Eleutherococcus senticosus (Eleuthero-Siberian ginseng)
– ginseng must be used carefully under specialist advice.

Lifestyle factors

Regular exercise is essential for the promotion of good health
in older age, and there are many forms that are suitable.
Older people should not, however, take up a strenuous form
of activity without a medical checkup. With any form of
exercise, the amount undertaken should be gradually increased as fitness improves. Exercise for the mind is equally
important, and older age should continue to be a time of
challenge and new opportunities. It is important to learn
ways of managing stress and to practise relaxation techniques. Other physical therapies such as massage, hydrotherapy and aromatherapy may all prove beneficial. Methods to improve posture and to correct any skeletal misalignment may be needed.